Table of Contents

To Brother And Ann

John 15:13

Dedications
Fins, Feathers, and Fur

COME BEFORE WINTER is a book about life's journey from an outdoor perspective. In life each day allows memories for another page in the journey. Each journey is another chapter travelled. Each chapter provides for more of the book to be written. Life is a journey. Live it so that your book may be written well.

I dedicate this book with gratitude to Chris and Wes. It has been my honor to have such memories and friendship over many years with these guys. Many of the antics are remembered fondly with "some accuracy" in the pages of this book. Throughout my formative years they were a big influence on my life and my love for the outdoors. Thankfully, with time and therapy I have overcome most of their teachings!

I would like to thank Scott and Steve for giving such great material along with their friendship. Thanks to Eric, a new friend. So many stories in such a short amount of time!

In memory of Dr. Harvey Howell: He graciously allowed me to use his property at any time without hesitation. He encouraged me, in many ways and for many years he mentored me in the outdoors that he loved.

In memory of Dr. Sam Howell: He was a fine doctor and outdoorsman as well.

In honor and memory of Don King: Experiencing excerpts from Don's journey was always fascinating. I learned to always expect the unexpected. But mostly it has been MY honor to have such a friend to watch when his journey became frightening and unknowing. In the darkest chapter of his journey, his unwavering faith and commitment to our Lord and Savior has been an inspiration… a true testimony to me.

In honor of my best friend, my son Joshua: My buddy taught me more about enjoying the journey than anyone else. Without him my journey would have been unfilled. His love for the outdoors pales in comparison to the love for his daddy. His love for his "pops" pales in comparison to his love for our Lord and Savior. Our time spent together is without equal and unforgettable.

In honor of my precious treasure, my daughter Lauren: She still thinks her daddy is "the stuff." I know better but I'm not telling her. Her love for her Heavenly Father is extreme …and justified. She has always allowed me to participate on her journey and that is awesome.

In honor of God's gift to me, my beautiful wife, Susie: Without her my journey would have been lifeless and void, with very little meaning. The colors of God's masterpiece of life were made vivid by His gift of her to me. Undeserving as I am I cannot understand why he gave such a magnificent part of His creation to me. Her love for Him gives me strength and completes me on this journey.

Lastly, but very most importantly, I dedicate this book in honor of our Lord and Savior Jesus Christ. He is the Master and Creator of the universe. He is the author of my journey. The memory of what He did for me through His death on the cross and that He continues to work in my life is the binding that holds this book…me…my life…my journey…together. Without his authorship the words of the sentences in the pages of my book would be meaningless.

COME BEFORE WINTER
FINS FEATHERS AND FUR

CHAPTER ONE
Commitment

"Wow!!!
"That would be great!"
"Count me in!"
"I definitely want to do that!

I've heard exclamations of excitement like those my entire life. I have on occasion uttered something very similar. I've known men who've spent countless hours making plans and talking about marvelous and wonderful undertakings they would do only allowing the excitement, like the dream, disintegrate before being realized. Somehow men seem satisfied with talking about doing something special, going to that "dreamed about place," watching, seeing, or hearing about adventure. Often they are found sitting around grunting like cave men and high fiving when the trophy buck or other on screen game comes into view. Quick to analyze and willing to offer the "expert," between handfuls of chips or swigs of sweet tea designed in heaven, a few pointers of their own.

There is more DO to life than that. Life should be, as the song says, "a little less talk and a lot more action." Life is a great adventure, a continuing journey. You can talk your way through it sitting idly on the sidelines giving others your "expert opinion" or live your way through it. Living it requires action. Living it requires commitment. Commitment coupled with action leads to a life long journey of mystery and unknown adventures.

A few years ago, a couple of friends of mine, Ted Perry, Sam Howell, and my brother-in-law Scott Mauldin, acted on a "let's do it" dare and planned a fishing trip to Labrador. Like a lot of guys, we had gotten together for a while on occasion and talked about "doing something." We finally came to our senses and agreed talking was just not enough. We would do it! Our commitment was firm! It was made firmer, however, by the deposits we each placed.

Our wild and exciting undertaking started long before we left. Unlike simply talking about going, we were REALLY talking about GOING. Our preparation and conversations now revolved around our foray into the wilds of Labrador. As we began to countdown the days until departure, we were already experiencing part of the adventure in anticipation. The unknown hidden wonders waiting to be revealed, the sights to see, and the expectations each of us had in our minds eye further magnified the excitement. All this contributed in helping to create and solidify the key ingredient for a successful adventure during the journey: a close fellowship. We had quit using idle words, and put them and our dreams into action.

Finally, the day for departure arrived. Our adventure had started long before we even left our homes in Cartersville heading to Labrador on our "fishin' mission." Getting closer to Labrador our mode of transportation got smaller and smaller until our final flight was in a floatplane. Our expectancies early on were exceeded as none of us had ever been in anything that could float and fly at the same time.

As the plane came to a halt, coasting the last few yards, ripples lapped onto the planks of the dock. Salutations were offered in the accented Labradorean way that we soon would come to love by two guides and a cook. They said we were the only people on the lake and for that matter the only ones within thirty miles as the crow flies. I reckon they were trying to bestow upon us a sense of awe, but at the time thirty miles didn't seem very far to us, more like child's play. We were not impressed with crows flying even if they were of Labrador descent. We did know, as a matter of fact, standing there on the dock, freshly emerged from the now floating, flying plane, were four outdoorsmen scarcely equaled by others, Canadian or not.

The guides explained it would not be possible to walk the thirty miles because we were in impenetrable tundra. Interestingly, it never really thaws out completely, and is covered with extremely old stumpy little trees that appear a lot younger than they are. The growing season that far north of the equator in the northeast corner of Canada is very short and the tundra area of Labrador, where our camp had been established is peppered with lakes and marsh. Sam and I decided of course WE could do it. WE could hike in Labrador. Probably even cover the thirty miles if a notion were taken. "What's a little tundra and marsh?"

One afternoon we commenced to trekkin' (roughly translated: took a hike). Forty five minutes later we were using our navigational prowess to ascertain our bearings while fending off the bird size mosquito bombers bent on withdrawing several pints of our red neck hemoglobin, each step a surprise, going over and around terrain that was either raised up by the ground or fell away a foot or so into the shallow water hidden by the lush vegetation covering it. Bushwhacking with extra ordinary precision, we turned around to take in the vista; there was the cabin, not more than a hundred yards away! We sheepishly returned not disclosing to the lazy ones our semi-defeat.

Staying at the cabin on this remote lake was no disappointment. The scenery was absolutely beautiful. Eagles, ospreys, and otters were sighted often, while mink chased and played not far away. Rumors and signs of bears were prevalent but spottings were rare. Innumerable birds and small game called the area their home. Abundantly available and eagerly consumed were wild blueberries, elderberries, and cranberries until our stomachs were content. We gazed at the bizarre Northern Lights: Strange and eerie glowing colors in the night sky. Also seen and heard in overwhelming quantities was what the guides proclaimed as the official bird of Labrador…

Perched outside the window and easily visible from the front porch was a huge replica of a mosquito with twirling wings that went around and around when the wind blew. As Sam and I had already discovered; the national bird, the mosquito, was in copious supply and thriving quite nicely, growing to outrageous proportions with appetites to match, rivaling vampires of ancient lore. You could hear the buzzing around you all day, as clouds of them descended upon you, escape was unobtainable, matching you move for move, avoiding swat after swat, allowing you no way to hide.

Some of our lunches were at lake side, grub cooked to please with all the fixins'. We saw no other people during the entire week. All of our water, including what we drank came directly out of the lake. A generator furnished power and a wood burning stove provided heat. We fished, slept, and ate, when we wanted and as much as we wanted.

We brought with us the knowledge that the victory in fishing is not limited to having to catch something, although that is certainly a bonus. In addition, the real JOY of fishing as in life comes from the events during the journey. Though we agreed to the statements more so in theory than action, we also agreed non-fishing members of our species more than likely perpetrated the concept. I have heard of other people fishing and not catching a single fish and still having a great time. I do not recall ever personally having such a fishless experience but I am sure some of my so-called friends could fabricate a story or two. This was not one of them.

One evening we consumed some of the fish we had caught. Generally it was catch and release fishing. The exception to the rule was allowed for "fish night " Every day of the week each and every week had one of seven desig-nated menus. Often the men would know the day of the week by what was on the "menu" for the evening or in remembering what had been prepared the night before. It seemed boring to them, but I can tell you every meal was superb. One of the fish we ate that night was a Northern Pike, compliments of Sam. These predatory fish, called the wolf of the north, are ravenous and have many huge razor sharp teeth.

We were warned not to reach in to the water to retrieve our hooked fish or fouled lures lest out of the murky depths would arise the forever hungry Pike to latch on to his newest opportunistic meal, leaving the unfortunate fisherman able only to pull back a finger-missing nub. The Pike we ate that night was one Sam had caught, or maybe I should say the Pike had caught Sam.

While fishing from some smooth boulders along the shore earlier that morning, Scott, Ted, and I saw some strange behavior coming from Sam's boat. "What IS he doing?" was the question on everyone's mind. He was swinging a big stick or bat or something wildly at the bottom of the boat. We soon realized exactly what he was doing.

Being the excellent fisherman Sam was, Sam had caught a Pike. Being the excellent fish the Pike was, the Pike had caught Sam. The wiry one-handed bat-wielding fisherman was busy trying to convince the fish to release his teeth filled, vice-like jaws from the increasingly painful meaty part of his other hand. Sam finally won but I'm not so sure it was much of a victory.

That night the Pike was very tasty. It makes for a great story. The title should read "Eating the fish that ate you first". The fish got the first bite of Sam. We bestowed upon Sam the honor of eating the last bite of the fish. It was, by the way, quite tasty!

At night, after a long day fishing we sat around the old wood burning stove and told stories and lies, usually one in the same, as truth never got in the way of a good story. Sam in particular would say, "Have I told you this one?"

It didn't matter if we'd heard it or not, he'd tell us again anyway. We'd heard the spiels before, and every other story, whether Sam's or not, had a familiar sound to it, but we listened just as intently each time. No matter how often they were repeated the legendary accounts came gushing forth with the same enthusiasm as if they were being told for the very first time. Sometimes Sam wouldn't remember which rendition he had already told. The same yarn, this time with different lies supplying the bulk of the tale, came alive anew. The stories told would conjure up shared sights and sounds, even the smells of the event seemed to return. Sometimes…well most of the time, as he told the story, the saga grew bigger than life. Then we would call him on it: "That wasn't the way you told it last time."

At other tellings, we would finish the narration for each other. We didn't care how many times we'd heard them, it wasn't about the story, it was about taking the time to fellowship, sharing our common experiences and life's stories, spending time together and lifting each other up.

In the mornings, we would be back at it: on a five-mile wide lake, formed by ancient glacier melt, meandering as a river the last few miles to empty into the ocean, hard at work fishing for football sized Brook trout and "the trash fish" Pike. The fishing and scenery were unbelievable! I was the type of place I had dreamed about, read about, and heard about my whole life. I never thought I would get to see or experience it.

While sitting on the front porch studying the "national bird of Labrador" we noticed something that looked out of place. Scott asked one of our guides what it was.

"A bear trap. It's to keep bears from coming into the cabin."

The "trap" was a sheet of plywood with huge nails driven through it every three to four inches. The points of the nails faced up. If you happened to misguidedly step on it, the nails would penetrate deeply into your foot and out the other side.

"What exactly do we do if a bear comes by?" was asked.

The guide said matter-of-factly. "Well you're not real likely to see a bear although there are several in the area. If you see a black bear act big, mean, and tough and you can scare them off and they'll run away. But… if you see a brown bear… you have to be quiet …AND very… very…still…Cover up and act dead".

("Easy to do, huh, with a brown bear coming" I thought.)

"OK. Sounds like a plan…BUT…What do you do if you're out here fishing at twilight, a bear comes by and you don't know if it's brown or black?"

The guide looked quizzically at each of us before he said "I wish you hadn't asked me that. I REALLY DO NOT KNOW! But that question will bother me the rest of my life."

Funny? Not real sure, but we all laughed!

Another afternoon we were fishing back at the big rocks along the side of the lake. The shallow lake was easy to wade, but it was black with tannic water so it was difficult to see where to go either boating or wading. Sam had a fish on his line. "Fellas, it's a big 'ole trout" (of course all of Sam's were a big 'ole something) and while he was working the fish in, he took a couple of awkward steps forward and went right into the water, more precisely, under the water. All we could see were hands, arms and a fly rod, but neither fish nor composure was lost. He simply kept walking to the next rock and landed the finned aquatic invertebrate. We all had a great belly laugh at his expense. He'd put on a real show, a sight to behold! He looked like a wet noodle balancing on one foot with a fly rod and hat in one hand and a fish in the other; we loved it. He loved it too by the look on his face and profound exclamation.

"Well boys, just another day at the office."

We made a lot of commitments on the trip, some good; some bad. Since Scott had earned enough brownie points with his "patient as Job" wife Sharon, he was allowed to go on this trip even though it was over his anniversary; though necessitating a phone call promoting his "unending love," "wish you were here," "be glad when I get home"…etc. (Guys, you know what I'm talking about). This commitment was a monumental task, requiring him and us to quit fishing early that day and was completed by Scott over a CB radio with a single caution from the guide: "It is a two way radio, all of Labrador can hear half of your conversation, anniversary or not, just remember that!"

Another commitment agreed upon at Sam's request was "No showers, boys, the entire trip until time to head back." It was slightly am ended when teeth brushing was considered separate from bathing, therefore allowed. By midweek we were not only "one with the fish," we were ones "as the fish." All agreed that the daily freshly baked cookies and bread could be consumed in whatever quantity deemed appropriate per individual without penalty or conscience, fish as much or as little as we wanted, and allow a little more "margin of error" in describing to the other boat either quantity or quality of fish taken. These are small fragments of my recollection of that trip. It was an amazing experience.

Before we left Labrador, we decided we were without a doubt, absolutely, positively, no question about it, definitely going back. We talked about it fervently with our friends through word and pictures. An individual calendar was made and personalized for each of us including our favorite pictures of the trip headlining each month in anticipation of our return adventure.

Unfortunately, we let talk quench our fiery passion for that adventure to embers and with time turn it to ash. We fell into our usual routine. All talk. No action. It's not that we didn't want to go back, we just NEVER DID go back. That was over twelve years ago. Sam has passed away. It would never be the same for us or the same four of us again. What had been promised by each of us to each other so passionately would not come to pass. At the time we were confident and sincere in agreeing to go back again and rekindle the flame of our adventure in Labrador. There was no question about it, but somehow talking about it just seemed to take the place of the adventure. Now it's just "wish we had". What if we had followed through on our commitment and returned? It's a shame we didn't. But why didn't we? The memories come alive in the telling but are overshadowed by regret of broken promises.

If you've read this you might think we were crazy not to have experienced Labrador again. You might ask "what did they do next?" My desire for you would be to stop reading about someone else and go have an exploit of your own. However, just in case you are not convinced, let me share why commitment and action in life and especially in men's lives is critically important throughout life's journey.

Adventure is about going for the goal, aiming for the mark. Not just watching it on TV, or listening to other people talk about what they did or what they would like to do. Notice I said going for the goal and aiming for the mark… not achieving the goal or hitting the mark. It may seem like semantics, but "achieving the goal" and "hitting the mark" seem to signal the end, more as if you finished and are not continuing. Personally, I have never been fishing and said or thought to myself, "Self, you done good! You caught one! No more fishing!"

Just the opposite is true. Commonly heard by my fishing buddies, my wife will readily tell, is: "Just one more cast, one more fish." Sometimes the extension to that utterance is: "That LAST cast wasn't very good, maybe just one more."

As my father in law would say "The fact of the matter is…" one goal leads to another and the mark is always moving. We should never be satisfied by our past achievements or by hitting the mark and then saying we are done. Adventure is more than that. Life is more than that. It is commitment to a continuous journey filled with exploits you take; some starting from the instant you begin thinking about them. Each day, whether great and exotic, or less exciting and boring, is an account of one's own life, and every day is part of an intricate puzzle, pieces interwoven, fitting together perfectly until the exact picture designed by the Creator of the universe is completed, the earthly journey is finished, and the eternal one begins.

Have you made any commitments to friends, family, or maybe co-workers to do something, only to fail to follow it through? Commitment involves a choice followed by action, being uncommitted, by default, actually commits you to something else. Uncommitted "sitting on the sidelines" is not nearly as exciting as being in the game, casting the line, or firing the shot.

In life, be very careful what you become "uncommitted to" by either choice or inaction....The consequences can be devastating and change the final destination of your journey. The choice is yours. I choose to stand committed to the orchestrator of eternity, the Lord and Savior, Jesus Christ, to lead my life's adventure. My prayer is that you will commit to take THIS journey with us so that you, too, have a story worth telling.

CHAPTER TWO
Boone & Crockett

or......

BONE and CRICKET?

In the hunting and fishing world there is a scoring system called Boone & Crockett. This system is named for two mighty frontiersmen, old mountain men, bigger than life legends Daniel Boone and Davy Crockett. These two men tamed or at least explored much of the early frontier. Their stories have held the imaginations of many people, including myself. Could I have done what they did? I have often wondered how it would have felt to be them, start walking uninterrupted on a course never before travelled by another just to see what was around the next corner, not knowing what new and strange places or creatures you might stumble upon in discovery. That is adventure!

The Boone & Crockett system is used to gage and score wildlife: fish, deer or other game, based on measurements of antlers, horns, length, weight or various combinations. Specimens taken are judged from the results of these calculations and are worthy to be called a Boone & Crockett trophy by comparing it against others. If the scoring exceeds the previous highest number then it is called a record. There is much prestige in a Boone and Crockett award. Boone & Crockett recognition is very elusive. Many people HUNT their entire life….HOPING for a Boone & Crockett trophy. Many other people HOPE their entire life…. HUNTING for a Boone & Crockett moment.

Well, let me tell something a little different. There have been some Boone & Crockett moments during some of my hunting, fishing, and life adventures. Boone & Crockett moments are great, they are exquisite, but they are short lived. They're once in a lifetime or maybe twice achieved. But some of my best and most memorable times are what I call Bone & Cricket moments. This is a scoring system not quite as precise as The Boone & Crockett. It is, however, dominantly pervasive in my life and probably for most so-called "outdoorsmen"' whether actual or self proclaimed.

Bone & Cricket is aptly named. "Bone" is used synonymously for the boneheaded things we are capable of doing to others or ourselves. "Cricket" is used to symbolize the other half of the "award". Crickets are little chirping, irritating, increasingly noisy, incessantly aggravating little things that you can't find, but they find you, constantly grinding on your nerves until they're on your very last one. You can't seem to shake them. They can't be ignored. No matter what you do they're just going to be there. You never know when they are going to crop up, but without a doubt, they will. Such is The Bone & Cricket.

These "awards" can be created by us. Often they are evidenced from unseen forces at work while on innocent pursuit. Randomly, Bone &Cricket episodes created for others are manifest during our own Boone & Crockett accomplishments. Every so often in the wake of some others' pinnacle of success; their Boone & Crockett moment, a brief installment of uncomfortable humiliation is developed for us… a Bone & Cricket that will forever live in infamy. Bone & Cricket "achievements" are told with great zest especially when sitting around a campfire or remembered to close friends. Without provocation, they are recanted as the result of an unknown force reaching down into the depths of totally unrelated events, springing forth into our minds at just the precise time to bring the most embarrassment to the one the honor of the Bone & Cricket was first bestowed. Rarely are they forgotten, they are stored just under the surface of our consciousness waiting to erupt. In a lot of instances, "You remember that time when?" is the opening line first delved into upon a fresh encounter with a friend.

God equips each of us with individual abilities and attributes allowing us to glorify Him, love others, and show them His love in fellowship, some of the most noteworthy times occur during shared escapades, past or present and caring for each other. A few of the "times that bind" are Boone & Crockett, but most are admittedly Bone & Cricket. No doubt, you can tell the difference, but just in case you are having your own mental Bone and Cricket while pondering the meaning of it all, occasionally you will be reminded.

I would like to share some of these short pauses along the journey called life… It's part of my therapy. Some of these stories I'll have to admit are mentally discomforting because they are about me. They mostly occurred by circumstance, or being in the right place or wrong place; however you want to say it, at the wrong time, or as a result of the things I did. The whole point is; if you don't have adventure and don't pay attention and savor the experiences of life's journey you don't have a story. And that's very sad! I have been extremely blessed to have stories and experiences with friends and to be able to share these stories again and again. My hope is that the tales will peak your interest or give you a little enjoyment. These are anecdotal accounts of friends, hunting, fishing, and loving the outdoors, walking in fellowship; recognizing the signatured masterful handiwork proclaiming the glory, majesty, and character of the Creator in every step taken, every sight, sound, smell, taste and touch enjoyed in the world designed just for our pleasure. The stories represent some times spent "out in the creation" but the depictions parallel life. Look closely you may find yourself in some of them. If not, maybe one of your "friends" will point YOU out in them

Let me explain a little further using some characters from the greatest book ever written. Most of these were men of valor and courage, Godly men. They had fellowship one with another, most importantly they made a commitment of their lives to God. But after all… THEY WERE MEN. I will list a few, but it would be in your best interest to read the book yourself and experience the Truth contained in its' pages, the richness of the Word, and the meaning of Life so abundantly displayed. The characters are taken from the Bible, but like before, if you look closely, you may find yourself represented by them. They all had their Bone & Cricket moments, like us, but the best part is through encouragement and faith, they didn't stay there. In the end their lives were Boone & Crockett big time! We are measured not in part but the sum of the whole. Who we are is not designated by a single piece of the journey; but the outcome during that segment can forever alter our course, a Bone & Cricket or Boone & Crockett for good or bad can impact the ones around us and future generations forever.

Noah was a righteous man and had lived that way for 500 years! God asked Noah to build an ark.

"Ok, Lord. But what's an ark."

"A big ship, I'll give you the measurements, and by the way you need to grab two of every kind of animal and put them in the ark."

It had never rained up to this point, so for a century the neighbors thought Noah was Bone & Cricket certifiable crazy.

Noah was true to his commitment in word and deed and honored God by building the ark. It took him 100 years to complete the task to the specs given by God, including gathering animals two by two, an estimated 75,000 of them. Noah placed them in the ark, God closed the door, add a little rain or should I say lots and lots of rain…Boone & Crockett all the way!

Job was a righteous man. He lost EVERYTHING he had. His wife and friends said, "Why don't you just curse God and die."

The devil, who had ONCE committed to God, was allowed to do anything to Job but kill him, heaps upon heaps of horrible things that only the "fallen one" could conceive. Looking from the worlds' perspective: Easy Bone & Cricket, maybe twice over! Through all the torment Job never wavered in his commitment of trust and faith in God. He knew that that was all he needed, and THAT, my friend, is how to live a Boone & Crockett life, even when it appears on the outside you have nothing to live for.

Mary and Joseph were righteous and found favor in the sight of God. That is an automatic Boone & Crockett. Even so, Bone & Crickets pummeled them, trying to detour the journey they were chosen to complete.

Mary was unmarried and pregnant (Bone and Cricket), very pregnant, riding on a donkey, (Bone) on the road to Bethlehem with Joseph, her betrothed. According to law, Joseph could have had her quietly put away due to the pregnancy, but an angel of the Lord appeared to him (Boone and Crockett), and filled him in on God's plan. When arriving in Bethlehem, it became time for the child to be bornBoone), but there was no rooms available (Bone), except a dirty livery stable (Bone). Through their obedient choices during their lives, Mary and Joseph celebrated with all of creation the birth of the Lord and Savior, Jesus Christ…. And there has never been a time better than that, or a Greater story ever told.

CHAPTER THREE
The Stories

The stories "fixin to be tol" pale in comparison to any stories in the bible, although there are some theological truths in them if you look closely. There are no men or women of biblical fame on the pages, but the funny thing about God is He takes the ordinary and makes it extraordinary, uses simple, but willing people to become rulers and kings, and uses His Word to forever change a life. Every story told is in honor or memory of the people and events, but more so in praise of the One who makes everything possible.

A few years ago, I was deer hunting in Paulding County with my lifelong friend, Wes. We had gotten up early, planned our strategy for the day, ate breakfast, and accomplished the walk-in to our prospective sites before sunrise. It was not too cold for me that morning as the walk had warmed me up just enough to keep me toasty without shivering or sweating. I felt confident. I had hunted that area before and knew it had deer. In a little while the world woke up with a vibrant sunrise. It was a still quiet morning. Yet, if an effort were made, nearly imperceptible sounds started filling the stillness. The songs of the birds and the scurrying about of the animals were greeting God with a "Good morning" that can only be noticed if you stop and listen, causing an understanding a little more clearly of the Bible when it says, "God spoke in a still small voice." Everything about the morning testified to the majesty and glory of God.

It wasn't long until I heard another sound, one I had been anxiously awaiting. The goal and target was stepping ever so slowly in my direction. In haste, I moved, looked up, saw the deer, and shot. The only problem was the deer had seen me first. I didn't make a good shot. By the time I shot, the deer was already running. Dumb, dumb, dumb. I knew I had not taken a good shot and should have waited. I had plenty of opportunity and time. I was just too excited and made a mistake, sending my misguided projectile forward, at best a wounding shot. The elusive one was hit, but only because of my super shooting ability and nimbleness of dexterity to pull the trigger lightning fast.

I tracked the deer and when seeing it, took another wayward attempt at the fleeing quarry. He kept going… I kept tracking. I would catch a random glimpse of him between branches and limbs. He maintained a slow but steady gait. I shot, he quickened. I shot, he ran, and then stopped forty yards away and broadside. Finally! I took careful aim, and was awarded with "Click"…. out of bullets! I had tracked the deer for probably a mile, and shot several times, at least as many bullets as I had in my pocket, some attempts had been out of frustration, some from thinking I had a good shot, but all to no avail.

Unknown to me, my "buddy" Wes had been sitting on top of the ridge watching all this with some amusement. Since our prowess as hunters was always the topic of great controversy around camp, this was a great opportunity for him. Each of us would try to "one up" the other, always trying to prove we were THE hunter, better tracker, better woodsmen, and sometimes better storyteller. He came up beside me and with a broad sly smile on his face, said "Would you like to use my gun, maybe a bullet or two? Or maybe you need me to shoot it for you."

That was all it took. I had fallen victim to my own inadequacies. There was no explaining my way out. Wes had witnessed first hand the course of events leading up to this indignant set of unfortunate circumstances. There was no denying it. I knew this story would be told. ANOTHER Bone & Cricket had arrived.

I reluctantly took a shot with HIS gun. That was the end of the hunt, but not the end of the story. It was told over and over and over, and unless I tell it, gets bigger and bigger each time.

Another time I couldn't blame anything on anybody but me. I was hunting at my house. Yeah, you got it, right in my own backyard. The deer had been especially bold. I thought "Hmm, why get up before daylight, trample all over creation, freeze, when you can just sleep in, go outside and "hunt"? I wasn't much in the mood for adventure that day. I just wanted to shoot something. The target and the goal would be easy. I would get right to it.

When doing something like that, just going after the target or the goal, often you miss out on the adventure. For me it's not usually just about the goal or target, mostly it's about the experience getting there. Having success without having to kill or catch anything is the best part, fellowship is the most satisfying element of the journey. That is a lesson my son Joshua taught me. The story will come to light a little later.

I had gone out my back door, probably fifty yards. There were three burger meat does standing in the pasture taunting me with their attitude. They were there every morning, no exception. So, I snuck up on them, took aim, and shot. Well, two of the deer ran, one stood there. I thought, "I got it. Great! Hunt over!" I waited. It stood there, and stood there, and stood there. Next thought, "I don't have time for this!!" So I shot again. Hmm…. I shot again, and you guessed it: out of ammo! I had only taken three bullets knowing that that was two more than I would need. I knew I could shoot that deer. I've always shot deer. I was a great shot. (Not counting my previous Paulding county debacle). But that deer stood there, looked at me and went back to eating. That made me mad. Since I was within spittin' distance of the house I stomped off, went back to the house and got more bullets.

I thought. "If that deer is going to stand there mockingly defiant, then by granny I'm going to shoot it. It needs to be shot. It doesn't need to pass on stupid genes to the next generation."

Upon returning, albeit a little bit frustrated, I took the deer with the very next shot. The hunt wasn't much. The adventure was terrible, but I had accomplished the goal, shot the target, hit the mark.

Now I could excuse myself and tell you that that was the first time I had shot with my glasses on and blame missing on the glasses, blame it on the wind or many things. But, "the fact of the matter is," I just missed. I couldn't believe it. You may think "That's not such a terrible thing, give yourself a break. Everybody misses," and that's true, but that's not the end of the story.

I field dressed, cleaned, and put it in the freezer. That afternoon Joshua came home, found me, and said, "Daddy, I need to show you something." Uh Oh!! With a young teenage boy you never know what "I need to show you something" means.

Spoken timidly the words came out with great trepidation
"Okay, son."

He took me to the bedroom and said, "Look at this?" I immediately knew what it was. "Someone has shot my window, door, and wall."

When I looked, my heart dropped trying not to believe what I saw. Standing there nauseated; mesmerized by the surreal sequence of events, though not transpired, thoughts played in slow motion the ramifications of the near consequences of my earlier actions.

In haste for the target, not the adventure, in boldness, and "superior" thinking, not only had I missed the deer … I shot the house! Had Joshua done the same thing, he would not have hunted for a year. Thinking back over it, I could not believe it was possible. The whole reason for hunting and past experiences told me it is not about "the kill," moreover; there are rules that absolutely must be followed. Never aim toward a house and shoot only where and when you know it is safe. I didn't obey any of that. That was a terrible time for me.

We can choose our actions. The consequences we cannot. Had Joshua or anyone been in the room, the resulting outcome of MY conduct could have been more severe.

I was fly fishing with my wife at a most beautiful place: Yellowstone, Big sky country. The unique land of diversity and landscape. Void of partaking in the experience first-hand, it cannot be adequately expressed in words. A land described as fire and ice. Frigid waters teaming with fish cascade through mountains and valleys rich in abundant plants and trees and all manner of creatures. Insects at times so numerous they create shadows as clouds. Grizzlies with cubs foraging for berries and grubs in anticipation of the next big meal, while Buffalo stampede across vast expanses. Sights, sounds, and smells. The bugling of elk join the lonesome howl of a wolf echoing over fields fragrant with blossoms of wildflowers contrasting the pungent odor of sulfur belching from deep within the earth's crust, as boiling water habitually and and faithfully spews from water-filled chasms formed long ago are considered common occurrences.

Being there you can really feel and see the magnificent hand of God at work showcased in unbelievable beauty and power, a thought provoking teasing of the senses, though laying dormant deep within like a steam filled geyser, a yearning waiting to burst forth and come alive that can only be awakened by experiencing it in person. Great adventures wait in a great place. It is "somewhere to experience," "something to be done": the place of Yellowstone.

It was mid-summer in the park, an awesome time of the year, with flowers in full bloom, rich grasslands hued deep green, rivers running full and fast, clear and cold. The weather in the park this time of year is fickle. It can change from freezing cold to burning hot in a matter of hours, but that day everything was perfect. It was a GREAT day. We were fishing on the GREAT and mighty Madison River, rich with history and GREAT numbers of fish. The sky was bright and clear like only big sky country can provide. My wife, Susie, was (and is always) stunning. She is a gift from God, one of His most marvelous and beautiful creations. The water of the Madison was as clear as glass and would easily take your breath if you happened to get in without waders or cramp your hand with just a brief encounter. Nearby, we saw elk along the bank, buffalo crossing the river in front of us, and a multitude of birds including the fish hawk. I was enjoying all this beauty and feeling pretty good about fishing the Madison River with my fly rod. I knew I was surely impressing Susie by my skillful application of fly fishing prowess. I was on top of the world!

Funny thing about feeling like you are on top of the world. There is a whole lot more under you than above, and once at the pinnacle of the pile, there is no where to go but down. This was one of those days.

Our guide was a stoic fellow. He knew a lot about this GREAT river and where the GREAT fish would be. He really wanted us to catch some of those GREAT fish, so he decided to take us to a special GREAT spot he knew about in an off channel of the river.

I was thinking "I'm on top of the world! I'm a GREAT fisherman in a GREAT place! We're on a GREAT river! I've got a GREAT wife! Our guide is taking us to a special GREAT place... HE MUST BE GREAT!" All of the GREATS were there except for the great fisherman part.

As we got to "the spot," the guide said "See that overhanging branch? Just below that is a big brown trout. All you have to do is cast that fly right there and you will see a GREAT fish.

I said "GREAT".

I cast toward the fish... I cast toward the fish.... I cast toward the fish... The problem was, my best efforts all fell short. I went in a matter of minutes from a GREAT fisherman (in my own mind)... to a good fisherman... to a pretty good fisherman... to a maybe better than average fisherman… to a terrible fisherman, while trying to cast to that stupid fish. I made all kinds of excuses to myself. "The wind. Could be that was it."

Maybe "The water WASN'T SO GREAT where we were."

Or maybe "We are too far away."

Then I came up with the best idea: "Maybe OUR GUIDE WASN'T ALL THAT GREAT! With each cast he kept telling me "do this" or "do that" "Over there! Just a little further!" I tried a whole lot of things that did not seem to make a difference in the outcome. His fishing counsel began to become more and more insistent. I sensed a little bit of anger in his voice at my performance.

I thought, "This backseat fishing guide is mad at me. Well I'm kind of mad at him, too. Telling me to do this, do that… GREAT!!!!"

Just about that time, I heard a splash at the back of the boat. I glanced over my shoulder, our guide was in the water, wearing shorts, and barefoot and even though the thigh high water was fifty-four degrees, was walking to the front of the boat like a man on a mission.

He got to where I was and asked to see my rod. I thought "Oh yeah! That's it! There must something wrong with my fly rod. Maybe there is a malfunction… Could be a latent manufacturing error… Of course it wasn't MY fault. WHY DIDN'T HE SEE IT EARLIER?!?"

That is all it took. In my mind I was back to my former glory, a man's man, survivor type: rugged, fearless, courageous, a knight in shining armor to my wife.

"This will re-establish my status with her again. This will clean up the misunderstanding about the whole episode.

After all, it was ALL HIS FAULT! He should have seen it sooner and done something about it before I went through all this casting and casting and casting. What kind of guide was he anyway? Finally he did something right".

Instead, he never looked at my line, rod, or fly. He simply grabbed my rod, took one GREAT cast toward the fish… It was perfect, laid out just like it should, exactly where it needed to go. Did I say perfect? Like a picture it was! He didn't bat an eye. Just handed me the rod, walked to the back of the boat and said "Now catch the fish." I did… It was a GREAT fish.

Lest you think it only happens to me, sometimes a Bone & Cricket occurrence can be a pleasurable experience especially when it's someone else's turn. A Bone & Cricket moment can be most enjoyable, while it morphs into a Boone & Crockett memory at the expense of others, furnishing a lifetime of pleasure and a story to tell forever.

Previously, "My buddy Wes" "helped" by offering to shoot my deer, letting me borrow one of his bullets, or offering a chew of tobacco." My buddy Wes" considers himself unmatched in his hunting and hiking. HE considers himself a stealthy woodsy guy, one with the outdoor universe type hunter. He is truly, in his mind at least, Jeremiah Johnson's better part.

One morning he, Chris and I were hunting deer together in a pristine place on Pine Log Mountain.

I'll get back to Chris in a little while, because he too has given me monumental moments of hilarity during his Bone & Cricket rituals, but for now it's Wes' turn to supply an episode or two.

We were hunting together even though we were each at our separate chosen spots for the day. Our understanding, like usual, was upon hearing a shot there would be a convergence of the non firing participants to the area of the sound producing individual, to render assistance as necessary; tracking, carrying, field dressing, or just whatever it took to get the deer off the mountain, out of the woods and get the job done. This particular morning the great white hunter, Wes, had shot.

Chris and I both new it was Wes because of the direction of the sound, so we met up and started walking toward Wes. On our trek we heard a scream... A blood curdlin' ear bustin' death cry. We quickened our pace not knowing what it could be.

Wes was lying on his back, the deer only inches from his head. Had the deer kicked or gored him, crippled or trampled him? We didn't know. Was he bleeding, unconscious, mangled beyond recognition... dead....? Nope! Bone & Cricket moment! He sheepishly filled us in on the details. I will translate the story for you.

Wes knew HE had hit the deer, figured it was a good shot. (HE always figured it would be a good shot). He commenced to using his unequaled tracking skills, started following a blood trail, very noticeable at first, but as the distance increased it soon became increasingly sparse and had nearly vanished, only a little bit of what appeared to be urine spotting the ground was perceptible, if you were proficient enough and looked real hard and real close.

Down on all fours, camo capped head only inches from the ground; like a bloodhound now, no track could escape him; no leaf turned by hoof would go unnoticed. He was in the zone, on a mission: A hunter's hunter; tracker's tracker, bloodhound's bloodhound, ever so slowly creeping forward inching toward the surely non living quarry. It could not elude him, not this time, not ever. This mighty man of the outdoors knew where he was going. The master was in complete control.

Then out of the corner of his eye he saw the foot of the deer merely inches from his head. He screamed and fell over backwards, chest pounding to its limit, his breathing rapid and labored, difficult to catch. We arrived shortly after this…and shortly after the story's revelation, my heart was pounding and my breath difficult to catch as well. Chris and I were screaming also… but in a rather hysterical way, enjoying a Bone & Cricket moment thanks to Wes.

I have already mentioned that Wes prides himself in being a great outdoorsman. Actually, he is extremely good in the woods, and I think he could walk the legs off a Billy goat. Did I mention he doesn't like snakes? Not even a little bit. He might be okay if he saw one distantly first and gave it a wide berth, but would not be glad to see one "all of a sudden like". Wes and I hiked a fair amount in the Pine Log Mountain area. On one of the jaunts, we were crossing from rock to rock over a creek, just kind of enjoying the day. Wes jumped and in mid-air did a complete pirouette, changed directions only to land on a rock not originally scheduled as the primary destination. I had no idea how he did that but saw his motivation. There on the rock he was first going to light upon was a decent size black snake, harmless, of course.

Now Wes is a Georgia Tech graduate. In his mind he knew the snake was harmless, but his heart didn't see it that way. Instantaneously seeing that snake and calculating his trajectory, speed of travel, distance to impact, and possibility of an encounter with the slithery kind left Wes doing physical maneuvers that would shock Ringling Brothers. It was a great moment for me.

Chris is another best friend. I've known him as long as Wes. He's the kind of friend you can end a conversation with and not see for a long while. Upon meeting, the conversation could resume right where it left off, like it had been paused to take in a breath or ponder a new thought or comment. Like Wes, Chris is a close friend, and that makes his Bone & Cricket escapades enjoyable, maybe exquisite, thinking about them is as if they just happened. That's the way it always is when a story is retold. The memories are revived to live again complete with vivid freshened details, pulling you into wanting to live them even more.

Sometimes when we would go on one of our risky ventures, it really was like Larry, Curly, and Moe. Frankly, we all were Moe on occasion, often though I must admit our actions identified us with one of the other two, not that being Moe was all that great either. One particular outing found us in Mountaintown, nestled in the Cohutta Mountains. Just the words Cohutta or Mountaintown bring back many fond memories. Hunting, hiking, fishing, and just fellowship and camaraderie filled the days. Many times the campfire stories and antics delayed getting our much-needed sleep and prolonged the nights. I feel like I grew up in the Cohutta Mountains with these guys. We would fish many of the rivers and tributary creeks, each one a different story and challenge. When we got the opportunity to spend a weekend or a few days, our favorite spot to stay was at some property owned by Wes's uncle Dr. Harvey Howell. The property was nestled in the foothills of the Cohuttas along Little Mountaintown Creek. We could catch trout, crawdads (crayfish to some of you), gig frogs, hike, and hunt.

Our camp and I use the term loosely, centered around an old Bartow County school bus. The bus was really an old, old, school bus, circa roman numerals for the license plate.

Our beds consisted of old hospital type army cots. Did I say old? I meant ancient, decrepit, old cots. I think they may have been left over from the Civil War, having been purchased used at that time.

The bus had a few remaining windows but no back door, no tires, or engine, just a shell of the bus it once was. No longer did it serve the purpose of its design, but for us it was more valuable than a Rolls Royce.

Once, in the middle of a starless, windless, pitch-black threatening night I awoke to hear something walking around outside the fortress of our hope, the bus. It had been raining earlier in the day so it was easy to tell something was out there, something big. None of us moved! Inside there was dead silence, not even so much as a squeak from the ancient rusty cots as the group laid there cocooned in their sleeping bags. Not a word was spoken. None of us knew if anyone else heard the slow, rhythmic, purposeful steps taken outside on, the cold… wet… ground….

Now most of our food and all of our snacks were kept toward the front of the bus, sorta' where the door would open if you were getting out, that is IF the door could indeed be opened, since it had been quite some time since it did anything but rust. The front of the bus was probably the most "secure" portion of the bus. Unlike the totally absent windows toward the back of the bus, more of the "windows" in the front of the bus resembled frames that were holding together cracks or panes of nearly opaque glass allowing light to force its way through the myriad of holes in them. The door still had some integrity albeit rusted. Secure is probably not a good word to describe the forward sleeping accommodations but mostly it didn't get as wet near the front of the bus when it rained and, therefore, was the best place available to keep our supplies out of the weather.

The hidden entity was trying to get at the food and it was BIG. It was ever so slightly pushing, trying to get the doors of the bus to open, the only obstacle between it and the treasure it was so intently committed on commandeering. "Good luck with that," I thought, doubting it would be possible to pry those doors open with a crowbar or good winch; dynamite would only serve to further destroy the remnant of windows. After the thwarted attempt at gaining access to the food stash, it left. The departure was fortuitous for me, since I had been sleeping next to the grub. At this juncture in time there was not a fiber in my being that was not on RED ALERT, but I was somewhat relieved realizing it had given up on the long petrified excuse of a door and was retreating, probably going back to the quagmire of primordial ooze it had crawled out of, leaving the food, but more importantly, sparing me from certainly being torn from limb to limb.

At least I thought it had! I heard a few soggy steps outside and then a bump on the side of the bus, a BIG bump. A few more steps, another bump and the horrific beast was at the back of the bus…the OPEN back of the bus. Did I mention the doors on the back of the bus were absent, missing, no where to be found, see you later? They were in fact plum gone, just when they were needed like never before. From the looks of it, the doors hadn't been there since before any of us had been born.

Then it hit me… It's got to be a bear!... It's BIG!... It's out there!... It's trying to get the food!… There was no way for me to exit save climbing out the back of the bus past Chris and Wes…past that bear. I knew Chris and Wes, "my best friends," would gladly leave me there to defend the food or be the food. They could live with both choices. Besides; doing so would give them a great story, and, either way, I knew they would be out of there.

Another bump brought me back to reality. This time it was more than a bump. Could it be a step? It WAS a step… A methodical, slow, deadly, calculated step… a step… into the bus. I had had enough! Evidently everyone else had as well. Like a finely oiled machine, we all simultaneously sat bolt up right. Two guns drawn, one one million candlepower flashlight pointed with deadly accuracy in the direction of our fear and foe.

I don't know what the "deadly killer on the prowl" cow thought about all that light and hollering going on, but it sure high-tailed it out of there, stride by stride through the mud displaying a rhythmic staccato gait much increased in velocity, paramount to Olympic record accolade. It didn't take much time in the retreat, but took enough, however, to leave a round soft souvenir right on the way out of the door. Several of our feet found it before our eyes did.

On one occasion while hunting in Mountaintown, Chris shot a deer. Even a greenhorn non-mountaineer woodsy type could tell without a doubt that Chris had at least taken a try at one. Chris shot what he thought surely was a "decent buck," knew it was a "decent buck", and was ecstatic about his "decent buck". While shooting the "decent buck" he obviously had not adjusted his sights very well. Not the sight of his scope or the sights of his mind. He had failed to protect himself from the devastating effects of "Buck Fever". "Buck Fever" is a very well known malady in the hunting community. It makes a hunter see a "decent buck" when actually there is a "just barely" buck or instead even a doe. Since not only was it NOT a "decent buck," "at least a four point" as Chris related, there were no antlers. The "at least four points" had somehow mysteriously been replaced by two bumps on the deer's head, "just barely" palpable through the skin. "Just barely" able to be seen were still remnants of spots on the "decent buck," weighing "just barely" sixty pounds, not much of a "decent deer" and "just barely" a buck. However, Chris had in fact, gotten "just barely" too close to his scope while in the process of trying to get a better view while taking a shot at his "decent buck." Instead of getting a "decent buck," he got a "just barely" buck and more importantly for the story, what is affectionately called "scope-eye."

Chris had a complete circle around his eye with bruising and bleeding, an exact replica of the circumference of the eyepiece of his scope. Now it wasn't the fact that he HAD scope-eye that caused the deriding unfettered reply of others concerning his great deed. An injury of that type proudly displayed resultant from a hard fought battle can happen to anyone or nearly anyone. It was the fact that he COULD NOT hide his eye from the scrutinizing purview of curious outdoorsmen eager to hear of grand adventure.... a Boone & Crocket moment...of great deed... of his "decent buck." The snickering turned laughter then unabated guffawing that followed was way more embarrassing than the consequences of scope-eye.

Be careful what you do in private, less others find out.

Well Chris liked hunting pretty well, but I think he really enjoyed fishing most. In high school some Saturdays we were like professors holding a "masters of angling" school at the Barrett's house. It was a pretty cool place. The backyard had a sink hole full of fish. Our attempted conspiracy to drown some worms in the pursuit of the scaled nemesis one day proved particularly frustrating for me. For some reason, although trying very hard, I was catching very little, the consequence of missing a lot of solid strikes. Of course this fact did not go unnoticed to Chris, he was thrilled.

He began to wax eloquently on technique.

"With the proper technique" he would say, "it is easy to catch these fish. You just have to know how to do it…a matter of timing… watch the bobber…get ready to set the hook…"and on and on he went. He finally said "Just watch this! I'll show you."

Although it was not until years after this incident someone begin to qualify, quantify, and define what a redneck is, this would have been a good beginning platform on which to build a "redneck if" dynasty. Rednecks have always been, and are identified by having certain qualities and traits, some of which are manifest by specific actions and speech. It usually starts with: "Huh. Watch this." I'm sure somewhere in the "You might be a red neck if" category this technique of fishing could be thoroughly expounded upon, and would be held in a place of prominence high on the "definitely a redneck" list, probably located right after the section of fishing with dynamite.

He watched his fishing pole intently as the bobber started to twitch. Like a cat crouched ready to pounce he said "All you got to do is set the hook… Huh. Watch this!" Sure enough he set the hook.

From my vantage point, it looked a lot like someone trying to jerk a rug out from under an elephant, applying enough force to quickly and effectively flip him helplessly off his feet and onto his back. The hook was set in this manner nonetheless. He really, really, really set the hook. Out of the water came the bobber, line and hook traveling at terminal velocity en route to our unprotected position. Traveling past us the tangled mess finally came to a stop. After emerging from the cover we had taken lest we got bobber eye, enough courage was mustered to finally see the outcome from the jerk (truthfully, noun for noun Chris could be substituted for jerk, but that could possibly be misconstrued as degrading). At first glance it appeared that the fish had been missed. Upon further investigation however, it was discovered he had not totally missed the fish. Latched on the hook was a pair of Bream lips. No fish… just lips. We busted out in gut wrenching laughter. As a redneck would expound, "Never had I seen anything like that before….'til I seen it for the very first time". Never had I seen a better illustration of reason to disregard such masterful interjection of absolutely worthless fishing tutelage. Never will I forget that moment. Never will he (readily) admit it.

Sometimes you are unwittingly caught in a Bone & Cricket moment, or you create one for someone else. The ones you create can often be quite pleasant. Fortunately a Bone & Cricket awarded to a person or group can become a

Boone & Crockett for you, allowing the opportunity to measure and score the event based on how much YOU enjoyed it while scaling how much the OTHER didn't (how much misery they had), to look at it and enjoy the experience from the outside, not having to suffer the pain or ridicule of the whole consequential outcome.

As I mentioned the Cohutta wilderness area is a favorite place of mine chocked full of life long memories. Many of these images recounted are first lived out only to be recreated over and over again with each thought retrieval or anecdotal recital. It was in this setting, the Cohuttas, the great wilderness of the south, that emerged event sequences destined to be inductees into the Bone & Cricket or Boone & Crockett hall of fame. I call these precious occurrences double BC or BC2. Granted double BC or BC2is not very clever, but is easy to remember. The older I get the more help I need summoning up information; abbreviations without having to recall or spell the entire word makes it a little easier….The government does it all the time, at least that's what the FBI says about the fmr. CIA Dir. gone MIA while on assignment with the GA DNR.

The good thing about BCs and BC2s is that you really don't have to call them to mind with great accuracy. Ceremoniously keeping alive the memory, telling a story "to the best of your recollection" gives adequate room for margin of error, sorta like "one told from the pulpit" on Sunday; not the preaching of the Word of God mind you, THE WORD of GOD is inerrant and infallible, true and everlasting. I am talking about some of the anecdotal accounts shared in preparation, getting everyone's attention, allowing the parishioners to snicker and roll their eyes, then focus back on the TRUTH of the WORD. Recollections allow fill-in in some of the spots that are unclear or clouded by time or might just need a little embellishing.

I assure you that all BC's and BC2s I have written about are 100% unadulterated truth… as I retrospectively conjure them up. The names were NOT changed for protection.….THER ARE NO INNOCENT ONES!! Nada, zero, zilch. Others who are creators or recipients of these same BC's or BC2s might have a different summation of the events, but due to the traumatic experience, or need to gloat, their offerings might be a little different rendition of the same occurrence. The deviation of the story as they would tell it would obviously be errant and inappropriately misleading.

One such BC2 was purely accidental, rest assured, but created by me. "We The Three" were fishing the Conasauga River.

Chris and I were together as was customary whenever the three of us fished water that was reasonably small. This arrangement worked fairly well since Chris and I could readily share the water.

Wes, of course, was far too advanced in his fishing "adeptness and knowledge" (more like "ineptness and gnaw-a-ledge to those of us that knew the truth) to angle next to such fishing neophytes. That at least was HIS take on it. Chris and I both knew Wes was a pool hog, wanted all the good places for himself, and didn't want to embarrass himself exhibiting his inabilities, either 'angle' you accept is fine, Chris' and my perspective just happens to be unequivocally correct. One thing for certain could be agreed upon; we always had a great time. It's just when it came to fishing, Chris and I had a liar and one that would swear to it in our group, Wes only had a liar in his.

With me in the lead, that particular day Chris and I were easing along the river bank in search of our next spot of likely prevarication concerning numbers or size of fish. Unknown to me, quite innocently, (for real), I bumped into an overhanging hornets' nest.

Next thing I knew, Chris went past me whooping and hollering fast as a rocket. As I glanced back to see what in the world was going on, I couldn't see anything unusual that would cause such alarming behavior. When I looked toward our original heading Chris was nowhere to be seen. I heard bushes crashing, stomping and more hollering. That was all I needed. I was going to run too! When I caught up with Chris, he was standing on a big rock in the middle of the river, and must have been at least ten feet from the bank, however, not even a little bit wet even though the river there was about three feet deep. Seeing Chris standing there in the middle of the river, bone dry, balanced on top of that rock, I asked him "How did you do that?" Neither one knew.

About that time, I realized I was kinda' mad, because to get off that rock he was going to have to get into the water. I was mad because he was going to ruin a great spot to fish if he hadn't already, standing there hollering; ranting and raving, acting like a crazy man. I was mad about him being in the middle of the pool on top of that rock. Besides being on the rock in the middle of the pool already, I was mad because it was my turn to be first and I wasn't going to get to fish that hole. I was mad…. Madly laughing that is! Chris was mad because I hit that nest, mad because I wouldn't get out of his way fast enough, mad because he got stung four or five times and I didn't get stung at all, mad because I was laughing hysterically at the whole BC2. Chris was mad….

for an instant.

That was his perspective. There's something interesting about perspective… recollection is all about perspective.

On another outing in the Cohuttas "We the Three" were going to fish Jacks. Everyone who is anyone that is familiar with the Cohuttas knows about Jacks River. This whole area was simply called Jacks. No apostrophe just Jacks. Part of the largest wilderness east of the Mississippi, it has many wild and beautiful areas to hunt, hike, fish, and camp. Wes frequently went hunting, fishing, or camping there with his uncle, Dr. Harvey Howell, friends or family, cousins and uncles. Dr. Harvey owned some property surrounded by the Cohuttas. The Mountaintown property as it was called was one of them. That is where the rusty old, old, old school bus we stayed in on many occasions resided. Wes and I have hiked to the head waters of the Jacks from the old school bus. Wes, the intrepid, knew this area like the back of his hand, knew it better than his block, his house, his room.

This particular trip Wes was going to fish a creek feeding the Jacks. Chris and I, the two lesser fishermen and woods novices, would once again fish together. The plan was for Chris and I to head to the river first since the creek was upstream from where we would start fishing, Wes would continue on the ridge trail and then pitch off further along.

Fishing the Jacks was a physical commitment for us, leaving many times at 3:00 or 3:30 in the morning depending on which section we were going to fish, sometimes "sleeping in" and late start by 4:00 or 4:30, along the way stopping in Ranger at Doyle's Restaurant to grab breakfast and usually a small snack to take for lunch. The drive was an hour and half or so on pavement, then depending on which section we were going to fish, would continue another thirty minutes to an hour on dirt and gravel roads inhabited by the "whoopty doos".

The "whoopty doos" were washboard like ruts in the old dirt and gravel logging roads, mostly in the curves or steep places, formed from abusive outdoorsmen driving like ridge-runners on the way to and from their wanderings. The "roads" rarely scraped, much less maintained by the forest service, would make both you and whatever vehicle you happened to be occupying bounce up and down, and up and down, and slide wildly on the turns. Many times we would take Wes's truck. Three of us in the front seat of a Ford Courier was amusing. Chris's 6'4", Wes's 6'0", and my 6'2" frame took up all but a hair's breadth in the cab of that truck, with nothing left for margin of error, making it impossible for us all to breathe in or out at the same time.

After the drive we would hike one to two hours to get to the fishing, at days end doing it all in reverse, except it always seemed to take much longer going home.

The climb out was long and brutal. We loved it!

As we got to our departure point on this particular trip, Wes said, "Let's meet up at the mouth of the creek when we're done and we'll all head to the truck together."

Upon reaching the point on the trail that Wes knew like the back of his hand we went our separate ways, Chris and I to fish the Jacks upstream to the mouth of the creek where we would then join back up. One final instruction from Wes was "Just keep to the right," meaning stay to the right on top of the lead ridge and at any conjoining ridge bear right. This would put us above an area known as "Big Bend," a very beautiful place easily living up to its name, as on the map you can see the large loop in the river. It is pretty remote because the effort it takes just to get to the water in that part of the wilderness. Chris and I had never fished this section before and were especially excited to see this new place along with the opportunity to lie about the fish we certainly would catch…Invigorating! We would usually release these native fish quickly to help insure their survival, feeling a sense of respect and awe for them and the battle for life in the wild. (It's also easier to make the fish a little bit bigger; forget exactly how many were caught or match the catching with the numbers in the telling, when you didn't have the actual fishy evidence to measure against.)

Chris and I walked for a good while before hearing the river. Excitedly, we quickened our pace, finally seeing the river, but noticed our position unexpectantly placed us on a high bluff that ended abruptly in the river. Undaunted, that small glimpse served as a catalyst, exciting us even more in light of the remoteness of the area and the exotic wildness of the river. Unable to reach our goal from there as beautiful as it was, a decision was made to keep to the right one more time since that seemed like pretty good advice at the start. It really didn't take us all that long to reach the river from our first viewing on the bluff. After all we were seasoned woodsmen.

Finally! Fishing time!

Our enthusiastic arrival was doused somewhat seeing a boat on the river. How did a boat, especially one with a motor, get on this wild, primitive, remote river, this far upstream? Now that was very weird. Maybe someone had a cabin close by on a piece of private land along the river or something... Surely that was it. You couldn't get a boat with even a small motor up most of the Jacks we had seen before. So feeling the fire of fishing enthusiasm come back on us, we walked a little and began to fish. Not long after, we caught one....Thinking.

"Great! Here it comes!"

Wondering, "Is it a Brown.... or Rainbow?"....

"It's....a...Bream"

Revelation caused quick exclamation, "A Bream!?! How did that get way up here on the Jacks?" If there are Bream, we should probably walk a little further up the river since this is obviously a "Bream freak of nature." My hat was off to that super fish for being able to get this far upriver on the mighty Jacks.

So, we began to walk and walk and walk some more. It was getting a little bit late in our allotted time and neither had really fished much since access was not great and the water was not looking "fishy." It was slow and deep, void of runs and pools, a little murky and flat, not really the best conditions for catching the native brown and rainbow trout we were accustomed to finding. This was supposed to be trout water: clear toothbustin'cold, cascading, deep-woods, mountain water. Maybe we were seeing the remnants of a storm from earlier in the week, despite that, the water where Wes was fishing would be good, even in post storm run-off, the creeks cleared up very fast, so we decided to just go closer toward our rendezvous point, "commence to fishin,'", and meet up as previously planned.

It would take more than a four or five mile brush bustin' snake scarin' cliff walkin' multiple hour detour to eliminate our hunger for the pursuit, so we continued on "fired-up" at a pace spurred-on by new found zealous determination.

A considerable amount of time had been consumed walking, and a lot of real estate was already behind us as our discussion turned heated, while noticing the mountain really begin to leave the river, rising abruptly and a significant curve in the landscape began to take shape. We were just now getting to the downstream part of the bend, and were supposed to start fishing AFTER the upstream of the bend!

By the time of our meeting with Wes, he was already sitting on the trail with camera in hand wondering, "what took y'all so long to get here and whacha been doin'?"
He went on to tell about what a great day he had fishing, how glad he was that he had decided to go to the creek. He "sure was sorry" he told us to head off on that first ridge... meant to tell us "it was the second ridge to the Bend not the first," and how the "second bend off the road is when you should bear to the right," "blah, blah, blah..." "from there, even on the main road, you could hear the river...." "wasn't all that far..." "Actually puts you on the good water and into some really great fishing"... "Blah, blah, blah...."

Of course, he was remorseful that it was already too late to find us by the time he remembered how to go to the river once we had acted upon his small miscalculation.

"Wasn't nothin else for me to do really, but go ahead and fish" he added.

"By the way, it must have been a long way to the river from there.

"How was the fishing? I kept a few for lunch."

"More than a couple hours to get to the bend you say…?"

"Hmm, too bad we've got to go"….

"I really caught plenty and the water just seems better and better from here"….

"Well, let's get started, time to go…." "MAN!! You guys really look tired. Want me to show you the shortcut out of here?"

We were NOT impressed.

A favorite BC2 on the Jacks occurred by my hand involving my brother-in-law, Scott, before the celebrated Labrador trip, during his child-like trainee phase of fly fishing, and started after a short walk from the Jacks River Trail parking lot on the upper section of the water. A popular spot for hikers and campers, the river trail is very moderate in both elevation and distance, hence making for a fine day of fishing. This particular day we had decided to fish a tributary upstream of one of the more visited campgrounds. It wasn't a very large branch, so we were my turn, your turn; my hole, your hole, fishing. It was Scott's turn at one very nice spot, a particularly fine run deeply pooled with plenty of cover. To take a single cast into such headwater nirvana would make the whole trip worthwhile. I had fly rod envy! Just the opportunity to wet a fly in the magazine cover, picture perfect, trout infested liquid, would be the pinnacle cast of Scott's young fly fishing life.

He cast and made a spectacular "hanging cast". A hanging cast is putting the fly in perfect presentation ON whatever is hanging over the pool or run. Now the rules to your turn my turn, your hole my hole state:

Rule #1: If you can not finish your turn in the hole or run you started without jeopardizing the potential for catching a fish in that particular run, you shall be replaced by the nearest fishing person. (In this particular case it was me…always)

Rule #2: The rule does not depend on the size of the pool or number of potential fish available.

Rule #3: Once you have established your inadequacy to fish, you are finished.

Rule #4: You may even be required to allow the replacement fishermen, (me) to continue his fishing mastery into the next pool or run which was rightfully his in the first place. (This is a portion of the continuation rule numbers 5 and following.)

Rule #5: If I catch a fish I get to continue to the next pool or run.

Rule #6: If YOU catch a fish I get to continue to the next pool or run.

Rule #7: If I get there first, I get to fish the next pool or run.

Rule #8: I can relinquish my next pool or run to you in order to change the sequence if it looks like my pool or run is not easily accessible or if your pool or run looks better.

Rule# 9: Other rules may be added as the situations arise.

There are a few less exact rules like the first eight, but usually # 9 addresses other situations, and are ultimately dependant on who wrap winds the fly on the overhang, gets stuck too close to cast, looses or whips off the once secured insect imitating feather and string engulfed hook, tangles the line, etc. Since I knew the rules precisely, I was quickly able to recite them, and eagerly ready to make the cast to this pool of rarely seen highly anticipated trout habitat perfection. To the point, simply stated: "With expert precision I cast to …and caught… a 17 inch native brown trout out of "Scott's pool" from the headwaters of Jacks". It was truly a BC2 moment.

In his infancy prior to Scott's childhood fishing phase, we talk about, and he freely admits to, another double

BC incident. I was professorially trying to teach Scott the fine art of fly fishing. He was woefully learning. I decided to take him to Cooper Creek. Now Cooper Creek is a "puts" and "takes" creek. The DNR "puts 'em in" and we "takes 'em out". You do not have to be a highly skilled extremely proficient fly fishing machine like myself on Cooper's. You can even be like Scott and catch fish. The trout are affectionately called "creek chickens," raised in pens from eggs, fed, nurtured, and cared for prior to being released. They are not the sharpest fin in the creek, but they are none the less fun to catch and good to eat.

I was very patient, and over the course of some time, I was expertly instructing like Lefty Kreh, Bill Dance, Roland Martin…, or me. (The same me once infamously revealed on the Madison River I might add). I would gently coach and quietly, lovingly coax Scott along with reassuring words and thoughtful heart-felt instructions of technique. He was amazed! I kept telling him that one day he, too, would be able to fish like I was demonstrating, IF he kept practicing, and practicing, and practicing. I was nothing but a kind, considerate, gentle being, whose very purpose was to reveal the world of fly fishing before the wide eyed impressionable tenderfoot. At one point, we got to a pool and I kept saying in my nicest way possible "A little further, and a little to the left." He would cast, and again would repeat myself and say "A little further and a little to the left". After about the third time, Scott said "Okay if you think you can do so much better, just go ahead and do it." For some reason he felt my tender soothing words had come across as mockery, hidden with condescending overtones.

My heart was heavy. However could he have thought that? I didn't know. Maybe it was the laughing and snickering or shaking my head or something like that during the day. He readily admits the events leading up to this point, maybe not fully comprehending the benevolent manner that was being implemented on his behalf, nonetheless, the facts remain.

He affirms that I had said "A little further and a little to the left." After a couple more tries and a couple more furthers and to the left he said "Why don't you just do it?" So, I did, easily and swiftly procuring another pretty nice 12 inch Rainbow that had been just a littler bit further and a little more to the left.

Just because you have been through infancy or child-hood fly fishing doesn't mean you can't have a BC or BC2 moment in your more "mature "days. Scott was growing up. Just when you think you have progressed, however, you may succumb to a sudden relapse.

He and I were fly fishing on the Hiwassee River in Tennessee, wading in a beautiful catch and release section of the river known as The Steps. On one particular shoal, I tied on a number sixteen Prince Nymph with a strike indicator in some fast water.

Scott laughed at me and said "Where did you get the bobber?"

As the words reached my ears, my heart changed the meaning from what was spoken, I politely and softly corrected him in my usual docile articulate manner indicative of our relationship, gladly aware of our kindness to each other. Someone else not understanding the highly evolved manner of communication we use might misunderstand our interaction and think we did not hold each other with highest regard afforded through mutual respect befitting brothers-in-law. It's knowing more about each other's heart and the true intent of our words and actions; that we would never take advantage of an opportunity arising against the other and no matter what is said out loud, the real connotation is understood, hidden deeply in our very souls. In this manner we are pretty good at hiding the real gist of what's said from the interloping, snooping outsiders bent on spoiling the emotion of the moment; they, knowing the true nature behind the words, might think us soft. We practice this veiled meaning technique often, on occasion uplifting the other by pretending to do or say something stupid.

Scott continued to make fun of my bobber. I continued to catch fish. Stopping even for an instant, he would have remembered I was way past him in the fly fishing tree of life. He even comments about me being old and having "thin blood," "Grandpa", "way back when…" etc. He should have been eager to hear from "this old man" about the strike indicator as it is called by knowledgeable experts, why it is such a great thing, that I would as usual, instruct him, encourage and amplify his fly fishing manliness; and help him. That's my perspective. I'm telling the story.

Seeing the error of his ways, instead of giving kudos and reverent acknowledgement, all he said was "Can I have one of them bobbers?"

He finally caught some fish.

Sometimes we can have a Boone & Crocket moment all by ourselves. No one else gets embarrassed or has any claim on the outcome, somehow it just happens. A BC2 seems better sometimes because often your Boone & Crockett comes at some others' expense. Coinciding with a less than stellar performance for them you get to exceed because of their failings. A Boone & Crockett is more of a "Thank you, me" moment, when our excellence comes out and no one else is involved. BC2s of course are more fun to talk about because you get to brag a little and make fun of them at the same time, but a true Boone & Crocket moment usually takes place when no one else can help you, when the best of what you are is accomplished. In skeet shooting it's a like hitting a double every time, archery it's the bull's-eye, in fishing it's the catch after the perfect cast to a rising fish.

These scenarios usually don't just happen. It requires practice and skill, drawing from the knowledge and experiences in life that got you to that point. Sometimes it looks easy, sometimes simple, but often appears impossible to others of lesser abilities.

One example of a Boone & Crocket moment for me occurred during a duck hunting expedition with my buddy Steve McCombs and my very best buddy, my son, Joshua. It was always an expedition with Steve. Very seldom was a hunt simple or normal, and this characteristically Steve induced trait seemed especially true with duck hunts: stuck in the mud at the boat ramp, motoring our boat in a non-motor wildlife area, paddling the same boat miles breaking the ice to reach our destination only to find that we were too late and had nowhere to hunt. Although the "good" thing about this particular hunt was that the guys occupying the places to hunt felt sorry for us: they let us borrow some of their ducks so we could have our picture made… Definitely a Bone & Cricket moment. We've also been duck hunting where the temperature was near eighty degrees and got very sunburned, only saw a couple of ducks, and those had already been mounted on the wall. Some of these trips required traveling distances, some closer to home.

This time we were hunting close to home around a small cattle pond at a friend of ours named Charles Croft when this Boone and Crockett occurred. We arrived as always before sun up. As usual it took longer than we thought to set out our decoys…meaning it took longer than we thought for ME to put out the decoys. Steve likes to direct the set up and complete and perfect placement of the decoys from the shore, I usually end up placing the plastic duck look-a-likes upon the frigid pre-dawn water. That morning was no exception, and every step I took required extracting my chest waders from the vice like suction afforded by knee-deep mud.

By the time all the decoys were placed at Steve's command, I was absolutely boiling, very cold on the externally exposed outer body parts, but inside, sweating like a pig, and hurrying to finish before sun-up since the birds would be flying only for a short period of time and there wouldn't be that many coming over us. The more I hurried the hotter I got, and had just finished with the setup when Steve shouted "Bird! Bird!" Grabbing the duck-killin' shotgun, I stood up, saw the bird out of the corner of my eye, and swerved around to shoot as the glasses became immediately and completely fogged. Not only spinning around in my haste, feet sill heavily laden with cow pooh mud, consequently, I was heading straight to the ground while firing a single calculated "Hail Mary" at the unsuspecting flyby. Emerging like Swamp Creature out of the mud, I removed opaqued glasses so I could see.

One bird. One quick shot. One Boone & Crockett. The moment was, other than the memories, over in an instant. More importantly, and of long standing however, was Joshua thought it was cool and loves being with his daddy. There will never be a better Boone & Crockett for me than spending time with my son, daughter or wife... or you with yours.

A little older, a little wiser. Joshua still loves his pops! More importantly, he has committed himself to sharing God's love with others.

   I fell a few years ago and broke my leg very, very badly, definitely a Bone! ... (Corny I know but it still fits). Most normal outdoor activities like hunting, fishing, and hiking were impossible. For three months, I could not walk or even bend my knee. The wheelchair and I became close, went everywhere, and did everything together. However, we did NOT have fellowship. Fellowship does not happen just because you spend time together "doing stuff," fellowship is created. Eventually, by month four walking was accomplished with crutches or a 4-point walker. Four months of not being able to bend my knee left me needing a fair amount of therapy, both physical and emotional. (Therapy much different from the intense group sessions necessary after completing an adventure with my "friends.")

I was anxious to get back to doing whatever I could, and was not sure walking was going to be one. Ed Atwell, a surgeon and good friend of mine, prior to going to the O.R. discussed this fact openly with me. Fortunately I could walk, and what better treatment than to be outdoors?

An opportunity came up to go duck hunting shortly after I was released to start vigorously doing the rehab. Even though it was with Steve, I decided the trip would be great incentive to work hard strengthening my leg and maybe push me a little bit while being gone. I didn't know if I could do it, but was sure going to try. It was hard to bend my knee, especially clad in all the winter weather clothes, wearing those heavy Mickey Mouse looking boots, and getting in and out of the blind or boat was going to be difficult. (It was often difficult getting in or out of anything with Steve!) The exercise would be different sort of therapy, a good kind of hurt, and a fun distraction from the real regimen of care.

Hence, on this hunt, for my therapy, I became "the retriever," a good thing, since there was not a dog. I would go with the guide in the boat, help spot the downed (no pun intended) ducks and easily reach them from the boat. Our out of blind time was significantly shorter since going with the guide allowed an extra set of eyes on the look out for any birds flying near, also gathering up the ducks that had been shot quickly got us back to the blind to continue the real mission of the trip which was hunting ducks.

The blind is essential for success. Ducks are easily scared. Like most birds they have keen eyesight. Motion and color recognition are extremely important for their survival.

Sometimes a bird would be down after a barrage of

firing similar to Ack-ack against bombers of WWII fame. But, during the lull of the hunt, some of us being extremely immature, were known to abuse the good natured but nervously on edge rookie hunters and on occasion blurt out emphatically "DUCK DOWN!" a phrase holding connotation of multiple meanings.

In its most important form, it meant, "Hide. Birds coming." Often heard after one of MY shots would be "Duck down. Bird shot." Of course, all birds had been shot AT with birdshot, or in my case, shot WITH birdshot so you could say "birdshot shot bird" but that would be overdoing it just a little.

On the other hand, just to test the resolve of the group and keep their vigilance and much needed skill - honed razor sharp while scanning the horizon; a little "duck down" could represent a feather floating by from one of those birds shot down with birdshot.

The "Bird shot, bird down," meaning I, or on rare occasion, someone else, had taken a duck requiring a retrieve or at least an attempt at it, held the most importance.

During the recovery of the now floating, once fleetly fleeing supersonic fly-bys, I always carried my shotgun while in the boat. On a rare occasion, Steve or Scott actually hit a bird. On these sporadic singular happenings the "Bird shot, bird down" often ended up being "Bird shot, bird up and flew". The very motivation behind carrying my shotgun, foremost on my mind was unselfishly helping Scott or Steve with the duck they so terribly miss-shot. Though it generally fell to me to actually kill the duck on the retrieve, I would allow them to take credit for the ones I so kindly assisted with, as it made them feel better to have a duck to show at the end of the day. I did not feel the need to take credit for killing all the ducks, even if I actually did shoot them all either in the air on the pass, or during the retrieve for Scott or Steve. This allowed them to save face with our buddies and wives when the story of the trip became legend and was recounted to ears hungry to hear of grand adventure. This sly method of gathering the ducks became so routine even on other trips, that to this day Scott and Steve actually believe they have harvested a few ducks unassisted.

The guide and I were out to retrieve a duck that was shot. I carried my shotgun even though I knew it wouldn't be necessary since I was the one who shot the duck and knew it would not be flying. I took the gun anyway because I didn't want Scott or Steve to get their feelings hurt. They are very sensitive. I didn't want them to realize my gun was only necessary in the boat to gather the ducks they attempted to take when in fact they had poorly shot and merely stunned them.

On the way from the blind to retrieve the surely dead bird… since I had shot it, a duck came flying lowly and slowly over the boat. I had no idea what that bird was thinking, although "bird brain" literally came to mind, but I also didn't know what the guide was thinking. With the boat at full throttle, he turned loose of the outboard motor, jumped down into the bottom of the flat boat, grabbed my gun, and instantly started shooting at the duck. The boat commenced going around and around and around, speeding erratically in a zigzagging tortuous course through the decoys. As the boat was spinning, my head was likewise, trying to figure out what the heck was going on.

The guide shot…Turned around. Shot… Turned again… Shot again. By this time, he had clambered into the front of the boat, leaping past like a ballerina in camo, as the bedeviled vessel continued its ludicrous trajectory, still zigging and zagging around like a drunken cooter-bug. He must have realized the back of the boat was where he should have been, and more importantly; the boat was still careening out of control as he scrambled in that direction. The erratic behavior continued, taking him in three or four long leaping awkward strides perilously close to the edge, causing near tumbling out of the boat on more than one occasion. I had little compassion for him. My thoughts centered around "would serve him right to end up in the water after a stunt like that."

However, those thoughts soon turned to extreme compassion and concern for his well being when I quickly realized, clutched in his grubby little hands rested my still smoking, though now quite empty, shotgun. He finally emerged at the motor holding stern of the boat, regaining its control, by now the boat was not even close to our originally intended course. With his composure slowly returning, he remarked, "Why didn't you shoot?"

My simple reply must have overloaded him to the core of his being. "You had my gun" was my answer. These were the only words spoken until we entered the blind, although I thought about completing that phrase with "You had my gun, bird brain," but I didn't want to offend the ducks.

Some of the Fins, Feathers, and Fur gang with the ducks "I" shot!

On another hunting trip with Wes and Chris near Pine Log Mountain, "We the Three" were chasing the allusive deer. Chris and I had decided to hunt Hanging Mountain and getting to the top of it was no easy task. Our trio parked at the old saw mill site to start our journey to the summit. The forecast for the day was crisp and cold, very little wind and no rain. It was going to be one of those picture perfect days. We started our hike toward the appointed destination down the old road. It was in poor repair, but was drivable with 4-wheel drive if you were a namby-pamby momma's boy and needed to ride in a vehicle instead of utilizing the manly mode of transportation called walking. "We The Three" of course being such frontiersmen, would never stoop so low as to drive in, the mountain would be conquered one step at a time.

Occasionally a flashlight could be used sparingly or emergently, although we thought they were a little sissified. We were astute, outdoor savvy, expecting a clear night we would easily navigate by moonlight using our finely perfected night vision. Although rough, we knew the road extremely well, with creek crossings masterfully forded and mud holes nimbly and skillfully avoided by three so mighty as we. About half way to our turn beginning the bid for the summit, distant light became visible approaching from the rear, moving toward us relatively quickly.

While discerning: two lights parallel to each other at a constant distance apart, extremely bright, a very loud rumbling sound associated with their oncoming; we very shrewdly assessed the situation. After all, We the Three were college nearlies, one eventually finishing at Georgia Tech. Our combined years spent in scholastic acquisition and keen, uncanny, awareness allowed us confident and conclusive agreement that a vehicle was approaching.

We really did not want to be seen, wanted to continue being three of the best, nearly world renowned great hunters; able to survive in the wildest of the wild. And most assuredly, did NOT want to talk to someone weak enough to have to drive to hunt. They would probably want us to tell them a good spot to set up, give them some advice, or just be able to tell their friends they had actually had the opportunity to speak to the living legends of the mountain. We didn't have time for any of that!

The decision was made to hide, blend in like white on rice. Busting through the brush at full speed one after the other we high tailed it out of there. Wes was leading, Chris was next, and I was following in order to protect the rear and keep them safe should any misfortune happen upon us. We stumbled and jumped, weaved and bobbed, leaping over logs going through briars and breaking limbs that were invisible in the slight light of the moon even to our expertly trained eyes. We were ninjas of the night, nimble, strong, elusive, and feared by the puny. Lesser men would have easily given up. Lesser men would not have been equal to the task. We ran like the deer, mimicking their agility and confidence. Stride for stride, we were at that great moment, one with the mountain.

After some time we saw what we had been searching for up ahead: Two very large fortresses of the forest standing close together, big enough for three guys to hide behind. We would become the ultimate phantom prey, unsurpassed and undetectable in our concealment: invisible and ephemeral; fleeting like vanishing vapors, here for an instant, barely evident, and then gone from sight just as quickly. Stopping motionless, indiscernible, as the bark of the tree we stood. The lights began to come closer, and closer and closer. We were steadfast in our commitment. Our controlled breathing even after our near marathon obstacle course was barely noticeable, nearly silent, a whisper being emitted. Closer and closer they came… Then instantly they were on us.

Surely these guys were great trackers, cream of the crop, wily and clever, able to follow the wind. Surely, their hunting skills were supernatural. Surely, they would rival even us with our unchallenged and unparalleled abilities until this point. They came upon us. The lights were right there….

Although it appeared unchanged and ancient, someone obviously had moved the road to within inches of where we had hidden, all but imperceptible behind those two trees…… Momentarily, within inches of each other, we converged; the lights, the truck, and the hunters. The lazy riders quickly passed us and traveled a couple more miles, arriving much in advance to the place we were seeking.

Just in case you non hunter-fisher types think you are safe, that Bone & Crickets can only happen to the hunter-fisher men, let me include a couple of bonehead moments created by my "near" friend, Don King.

Don King's continually smiling regularly made me nervous!

I guess he could be my dear friend, after all, his best bonehead story has some redemption value to buffer the tumultuous effects of the first ones; so much, I actually enjoy telling the third one, and that is what friends are for.

Let us go ahead and get the caustic ones out of the way. The first one is brief but sets a solid background for reasons not to trust Dons' adventure planning. The second is more complicated and less fun to tell since I was one of several on the Bone end although admittedly it was part my fault because I listened to him.

Don planned a weekend dive trip, made all the arrangements, and even borrowed a cargo trailer from his cousin, a member of a gospel group, "The Dove Quartet" to haul our massive amount of gear and allow our vehicle to remain dry between dives and the drive home. Prominently displayed on both sides of the trailer was their name. We cleverly taped over the O, corrected the spelling, and became "The Dive Quartet" since we had four going but had not yet gotten wet. Coming back we would take away the temporary change of identity and return its former glory.

We left after work on a Friday evening. That was the end of normalcy...Needing to drive all night in order to reach our goal, we stopped only briefly for a take-out burger. A couple hours later, however our "Let's drive straight through so we can get a little nap before we dive" turned into "Guys, we gotta stop somewhere." I was really feeling pretty bad. "Mexican Misery" via a quickie burger was wreaking havoc. So we stopped while I quickly and literally ran, into the non-lighted, non-air-conditioned stinky truck stop bathroom on a mid summers ninety degree night, staying in there long enough for the proprietor, fearing for his life from the diving hoodlums, to call the cops. The misunderstanding was quickly resolved. Wish I could have said the same for my headaching, perspiring profusely, self.

We eventually finished the drive, but way behind schedule, arriving at our destination shortly before the boat was scheduled to depart. It was adding up and becoming clear to me, as I was scanning the dock looking for Gilligan, fearing the boat was going to be named the S.S. Minnow, as we were scheduled for a three-hour dive.

"No boats going out today guys. Heavy rains and terrible winds. Seas' too rough" were the words now pounding like a sledge hammer in my already been in the car fourteen hours, food poisoned, weary brain.

Don spoke up reassuring and smiling, "Don't worry, guys. This can't "dampen" our spirit. We came to dive, why don't we go to the springs? They're fun, only a few hours from here and they really are on the way back home, so that's good. Let's go do that."

I always hated when Don made an exclamation along the lines of "don't worry," especially with a famous big 'ol Don King smile on his face. None of us had even thought about being worried until Don said it, now we were scared!

Against our better judgment, we headed north toward the springs and although we would eventually need to head in that general direction, the springs were far west from a straight line home. Upon reaching the first spring it was discovered closed. Subsequent springs all were closed due to flooding and visibility. We never set one foot in the water. There was no change made to the sign. Two days driving. Two days of anticipated adventure thwarted. Two days wasted. Two days of typical Don.

I knew better. I had free will. What was I thinking? I actually chose to be involved. To this very day some guys and I, as well as some of Don's own family, second-guess their decision to follow him. Crazy part about it was this was not the first Don King extravaganza I had participated in, nor would it be the last.

All of us on that ill-fated non-diving dive trip loved hiking, backpacking, and camping. The thought of combining those three activities was making Don's new "grand adventure" enticing, suckering us in and must have been what clouded our minds. From the very first mention of the endeavor and destination, the promise of a remote location with relative solitude except for our group was just the ticket. Cumberland Island was going to be our highly anticipated terminus. I knew some of the history of this coastal Georgia island, the summer getaway homes built by the rich and famous, the early indigenous tribes that use to live on this island, scattered wild horses roaming on the island, and miles of unspoiled beaches. "How cool!" I thought.

Especially exciting for us would be walking to our destination and waving good-bye to civilization. To get to the island, reservations had to be made in advance and a ferry boat was required, no turning back. Once there you were committed. (Little did I know we should have been committed for being there with Don King in the first place.) I shuttered with boyish expectation of Cumberland Island and the adventure lurking in wait for us. Now I shutter when someone just simply speaks of it, you know…. "That place."

We were all quite excited on the drive down toward our new temporary encampment and arrived well in advance of our departure time on the ferry, which actually surprised me. By this time nothing had gone wrong! Maybe Don could actually make a plan and it go off without a hitch.

Gathering our gear we boarded the ferry for the short ride over to "that place." To most of the other passengers we were obviously going camping. Why someone asked the question I don't know, but someone said "Ya'll goin' campin'?"

"Yep" was our well-articulated reply.

Poor guy looked somewhat confused when we further explained we were going to camp in the back country.

"Really? Ya'll not stayin' IN the campground?"

"No sir. Not us" we replied.

"We're going to be real campers. All we need is right in these here backpacks. No need for any frills with this bunch. Even got our back country pass."

Then it hit me…. I never saw the permit. Unbelievably, Don had it! Another kudos for Don, he was really coming through.

We got off the boat at the city slicker sissy camp. It had running water and even showers. We sure were glad we were manning up and REALLY going camping. On that island, you know "that place," in the backcountry you had to take everything with you and pack everything out. My pack was fully loaded, not only with enough clothes and food, but also a tent, and securely lashed to the corners were four one gallon jugs of water, additionally perched precariously on top of it all, I might add, a 2-burner Coleman stove complete with fuel. Open fires were prohibited where we were going, so the stove would serve to cook our meals. My pack weighed in excess of eighty pounds and being top heavy, I needed help getting it on especially in the sand, but once accomplished, could carry it for quite a while.

We started down the trail to our paradise destination on the wild and exotic, you know, "that place." We were getting thirsty very quickly. I volunteered my water since it was conveniently accessible and readily available, and my pack becoming heavier a lot quicker than I had anticipated was in need of some fast weight reduction. A break for water would give me time to reconsider the situation a little.

After an all too brief rest to quench our thirst, my pack continued much to my dismay dishearteningly unwieldy. Maybe it was that we were walking on a skinny trail down the middle of the island with palms and bushes continuously attacking from both sides and sometimes overhead while in ankle deep sand. Maybe something psychological caused a glance forward or backward in either direction on that stupid little branch laden trail that made us realize we were plodding along a pathway that continued straight until vanishing unto itself like the horizon on the ocean. Maybe it was walking on that stupid little trail in the sand while having one of the aforementioned psychological episodes in ninety degree weather. Maybe it was all of the above plus the fact that I chose of my own free will to follow Don King to that place in August, South Georgia, middle of the summer, middle of the island, middle of nowhere.

We saw an opening up ahead. With renewed vigor, we continued…. through the dunes, knee-high sand, with no-shade blazing August sun draining us of moisture while creating wind-burned, sunburned lips. Way to go Don! Way to go us! WAY TO GO ME!

Several hours later, we finally reached our destination for camp, quickly set up and headed for the ocean less than a mile away. It felt WONDERFUL! By the time we got back however, any remnant of the ocean breeze or the cool water lapping at the shore covering us was gone. We were, however, covered in a kind of sticky feeling nasty cohesion of sand, salt, and sweat combining to form a uniquely putrid B.O. that could only be possible on that island in the middle of August.

There was a fresh water source marked on the map. The solution to the pollution, so prominently manifest from every pore on of us turning even the air rank, we figured was to go there, rinse off, and get some cool clear drinking water; inasmuch as the other water from the jugs was nearly gone and at "room temperature"-ninety plus degrees. We were now invigorated, the thought of clear cool refreshing water being pumped from the wellspring deep within the earth was painting frosty images in our minds. The pump was just as I had pictured, even rusty and red, with a big nozzle signaling plenty of water could be procurable in a short period of time. I do not know who started pumping first, but the water began gushing after just a few strokes…

What WAS that smell?.. All at once everyone knew our fantasy of clear, clean, invigorating refreshment turned into water from a sulfur spring. Sulfur water stinks, tastes awful, just like it smells, is cloudy like diluted milk, and is repulsive. The dream turned nightmarish water wasn't even that cool, and washing off with it didn't make you feel clean, more like a big boiled egg. Surely this water hadn't come from Georgia. We must have tapped into a spring all the way from Florida!

Back at camp not invigorated, we ate hot stuff. Middle of August, cooking over a Coleman stove, eating hot stuff….and STANKIN'….Thanks a lot Don.

After our hot middle of August dinner, Don pulled out a bag full of grey white powder, emptied it into a sock, and began to sprinkle it around his tent, chair, socks, and shoes.

It smelled like seven dust, which coincidentally it was.

"You need to put seven dust around anything that touches the ground," he declared. "Ticks, you know."

Ticks, mites, chiggers and other bugs in plague like numbers were the undisputed champions of the flora and fauna. We were considered new ripe meat easily attainable sitting on our chair logs. Not only were the ticks visible walking among the leaves and sticks, their tramping little legs in multiples of eight, times the untold thousands surrounding us were audible to the unassisted ear. Unbelievable!

Sleeping was nearly as fun as the rest of our adventure up to this point. The mosquitoes were on a mission. Their goal was to annihilate the new creatures through bloodletting by morning. Sweating profusely, bug spray was useless. We were lying on our sleeping bags with the tent as open as possible trying to stay the onslaught, hoping beyond hope for a little teeny tiny breeze to come to our rescue. Maybe eighty five degrees with mosquitoes flying in formation above us, ticks marching all around us, blending with the constant sound of sweat pouring from our bodies would somehow feel a little less like pestilence from the Bible with just a teeny tiny little breeze.

There was none.... Thanks, Don!

The next morning came …s…l…o…w…l…y…I think Job would have been anxious of its arrival. Don said it was "supposed to be hot today"… Glad it hadn't been hot so far! We did not cook. Regretfully, we mixed warm stink water in our instant packs, drank stink water, and brushed our teeth with stink water.

On the map was another fresh water spring on the tip of the island. Word had it that it was real water. A couple of the guys headed out to bring some back, the rest of us headed to the beach. We stayed there quite a while basking in the sun while covered in the cool surf. Leisurely walking the return to camp we tried in vain to stay refreshed and high spirited, but ended up sweaty and thirsty with only hot stink water as our reward.

Arriving back at the camp, we were greeted with some serious discussion going on. Some of the guys were not going to stay another night, they were leaving.

They departed in the "cool" of the evening, near dark, opting to go the long way via the beach instead of traveling that asinine mid island trail. The story goes, on the way back, they were going to take a little sit break on a couple of logs that had washed up on the beach. Nearing arrival, the log-look-alike alligators slowly slipped back into the surf.

We had so much "enjoyed" the day before, that, upon hearing this story, I, in a moment of weakness and for a fleeting instant wished Don had taken a much-deserved rest on one of those logs.

Scott, Don, and I (Scott and I were the real men of the group), stayed one more night in a beautiful area well away from our previous camp. There, huge live oaks and a fantastic breeze offered continuous enjoyment throughout the rest of our stay. The only episode that happened before we left occurred between camp and a walkway to the beach. A wild horse came running down the trail immediately upon us, stopped just long enough to steal the last remaining candy bar just opened to celebrate the next days joyful journey home, and continued along a journey of his own.

A few days after getting back, we all received a nice letter from the park service. In it mentioned the closing of the well after we left due to contamination. I thought frankly it was overdue. They also sent quite an interesting dissertation from the CDC about the record number of ticks that year on "that place," and asked us to thoroughly search for and numerically and descriptively document the number of ticks, while visiting that fine tropical paradise, which becoming attached, had escaped. They said that some of the ticks were very tiny, that even those tiny ones were important, could carry disease, and might be hiding in some very strange or private places. They advised "maybe someone ought to help with a thorough exam especially in places not easily accessed, possibly a friend."

My wife helped me… I don't know who Don King got to help him. He certainly didn't have a friend after that.

Another story recorded for posterity was the Bone and Cricket for Don, Boone and Crockett for the rest of us that I especially like. He really deserved it after … you know "that place", that unspeakable place we went. Don really loved diving. Often we would gather a bunch of guys and go down to the Suwannee River, Florida Springs, or along the Florida panhandle "black water diving" where visibility is more a question of IF instead of how far, hitting the bottom before seeing it on occasion was commonplace. We would have lights that were as bright as day, but once taken into the water, would illuminate only about eighteen inches to two feet. We loved this diving and looking for "keepsakes". Bottles, arrowheads, artifacts, fossils and all sorts of interesting items could be found in these places. Don for some reason usually wound up not finding much, the rest of the group would surface with a myriad of items…. Don would come up empty handed, maybe finding sleep on the bottom more enjoyable.

I called Don before leaving on one of our planned trips with some good news.

"Don, I got a Suburban to take diving this weekend."

"What?"

So I repeated myself, a little confused at his question but still excited about the new family vehicle able to take four or five of us and all our gear diving.

"I got a Suburban for us to take diving"

"I don't think we should do that. I'm not comfortable at all with that. Are you kidding or what?"

"I'm not kidding. I think it will be great. I can't wait!"

"Does anyone else know about this? Have you told 'em?"

"Not yet. You were the first one I called. As a matter of fact I was fixin' to bring it over and show you."

"Pam won't like it even if it is a joke."

"It's not a joke. She must really be a Ford girl!"

"What does that have to do with anything?"

"You know Ford Explorer, Chevy Suburban."

"Oh!...Now I gotcha!....I was REALLY worried there for a minute. I thought you said I got us some bourbon to take with us diving. That was weird."

I thought it not weird, rather the way it usually went, and both knew bourbon would never be a part of anything we ever did.

On one particular dive we all got up on the boat and Don was still in the water, kind of unusual for Don , who was normally back on the boat before or at least by the time everyone else emerged. Bubbles were moving so we figured he was still breathing. The dive site chosen was near one of the springs in a pretty good area of the river that would usually yield something of interest and we all had in fact found something to take home.

Eventually Don came up out of the water with a big grin on his face.

He said "Man I got a ton of stuff! I just stayed down there getting stuff."

Resultantly, our curiosity was peaked and we were now anxious to see what was clutched so tightly. He wouldn't let us see his "stuff" until we showed all we salvaged. We had on past expeditions found a crocodile or alligator skull, our buddy Bob found a Mastodon tooth, and I found of a cross-section of bone from a Mastodon leg. We'd find ribs and turtle shells and all sorts of unidentifiable, fossilized, ancient reminders of days past. He must have found something REALLY good. After we'd looked through everything else from the dive it was then the highly anticipated unveiling….It was Don's turn.

"I got a whole bag full of stuff."

So he started pulling out things. I was good at recognizing what they were, having looked at artifacts from "by-gone days" and had done a lot of fossil hunting before. First thing he pulled out was a set of car keys.

"This isn't too much but I found a set of car keys. I reckon those folks are still looking for their keys somewhere but I found them. I done good."

Then, "Look what else I found…."

"The piece de resistance!!!"

He began to pull out a LOT of bones. The more he pulled out, the more he grinned. Like a magician reaching into his bag of tricks, expression widening, he pulled out more. A BIG Cheshire cat look finally erupted on his face, and unable to restrain myself any longer, I started laughing.

"What are you laughing about? This is the best stuff I have ever found! The best I've EVER done looking for these fossils and all."

I said, "Don you did real well, but the only problem is you pulled up someone's picnic. Those are all chicken bones. Some of them still have some meat on them."

He had an overwhelming look of shock and disbelief on his face. He was really disappointed, but we all enjoyed it tremendously. He pitched all of them back over the end of the boat and kind of sat there all sulled up. We gave him a pretty hard time, but he deserved it. He deserved a Bone &

Cricket moment as partial payback for taking us to "that place" we went… that Cumberland Island. Other than Don, we were all quite pleased with the outcome of the "dive booty" shown to us, especially the ones who had participated in the "Island of misery" tour.

Don had notoriety for trips like Cumberland Island. When we would ask somebody if they would like to go do such and such with us, they would say "Is Don King in charge? If so, I'm not going." He had quite the reputation and worked hard to maintain it.

*Don had one more story, an adventure he definitely wanted told, about a journey he had planned for years. We often discussed it, told others about it and invited them with us. It's a journey of life long commitment and desire, there is no greater destination. It is THE journey of a lifetime. Although traveling on different paths, I will joyfully meet Don at journey's end with a great reunion. Don has been an inspiration to me in his life but more importantly in his death, always proclaiming our Lord and Savior Jesus Christ. Don went to see him face to face, and with many other friends, I will join them in fellowship. Don died Friday, August 24, 2012. He was indeed a good friend. He will be sorely missed.

One moment especially sticks out in my mind in days past was not a hunting or fishing moment, but was quite traumatic personally. It was a big embarrassment. In a flash another Bone & Cricket for me, but as usual there were more guys around who really experienced the true joy of the occasion. They had a Boone & Crockett at my expense.

In high school I belonged to an explorer post, an extension of the boy scouts, only older, more "mature' guys (supposedly). The activity we specialized in was caving. Spelunking is the official word but caving is descriptive of what we did, spelunking seemed sorta' wimpy comparatively speaking, and was definitely harder to say or spell. All the guys were members of the National Speleological Society, had maps to the caves around the area, and would spend Saturdays and some entire weekends all over north Georgia, Alabama, Tennessee, and into Florida, exploring these vast and twisted imperfections in the earth's crust. I was not the smallest guy, but was, however, the youngest by a few years. I was always in for an adventure while going somewhere different "to check things out", hence the designated gopher, mole, super mud crawler, sent searching for passages yet hidden. They would enthusiastically encourage me into "this hole" and "that crevice" to see where it might lead sometimes pushing, shoving or prodding me. If I came back alive, it would be alright for them; then, they would go. Many times I would "get" to check out how deep the water was in need of crossing, see how long or deep a hole was, or perhaps do some chimneying: climbing or descending with hands on one side of the rock and feet on the other over the unknown depth of an abyss.

In this particular cave, the opening made it intriguing. It was a pit. A rope hanging limply off the edge for descending into the chambers below had been tied to a car sized boulder at the top of the cave.

Wanting me to check it out, they cajoled me with "Well you know you don't really need your helmet since this is a pit. There ain't no rocks gonna come crashing down.

Wouldn't hurt nothin' no way."

Back then we had helmet mounted lanterns that were purchased along with a refueling supply of carbide at Hodge Army Navy store, just like the coal miners of old would use to light their way. Carbide mixed with water creates a gas that will readily start a fire or explode given the right conditions. We also took other lights, candles, and flashlights of several varieties so we would have plenty of illumination if one of the primaries failed.

But on this particular cave and this particular time they said "You know you don't really need much. It's just a pit and it's got a rope. Why don't you go down and see how deep the pit goes?"

So being a little naïve and not really thinking about what was going on I got on that rope, absent of helmet, which normally would have held my primary light. Also missing were candles matches or any other light source for that matter. So equipped, or ill equipped thusly, descent into the pit began, nonetheless The routine when using a rope is to tie a knot near the end so while repelling you literally know when you've "reached the end of your rope," stopping on said knot without plummeting to your death in a cold dark pit is advantageous.

I started climbing down the rope and at a good distance, discerned in my head and felt in my gut, "This is not a good idea…! Matter of fact, this is a BAD idea…! Whose idea was this, anyway?"

The entire scope of what was visible to me was the opening of the quickly entombing pit and silhouetted against a blinding, sun filled cloudless sky, the guys looking down on me. That was it! No sliver of light could penetrate the chasm to that depth. I also realized it was now too far to climb back up unassisted, the ascenders were still up there, and I was too tired anyway, down would be my only option. A few more feet and much to my horror there was not a knot at the end, my leg no longer felt security from wrapping around the life saving rope!

I was using the usual method of descending into the abysmal shaft of darkness, alternating sliding one hand down then holding, sliding then holding, sliding and holding, while wrapping both legs around the rope to aid in slowing the descent. Many a moon ago, that was a relatively easy task. Now I couldn't do it if my life depended on it.

I was still holding on with both hands but had nothing to wrap my legs around. My feet were dangling around desperately trying to find more rope or at least the knot so that I might find purchase and give a little relief to my tiring, aching arms and hands. With fingernails hurting and entire body screaming at me, somewhere in the background amidst the pain my whole protoplasmic assembly was saying, "Stupid. Stupid. Stupid!...THINK!!!

So, calmly of course, but using my outside voice I began hollering, "Guys I've gone as far as I can go. I'm out of rope. It's pitch black. I can't see anything. I don't know where anything is. PULL…ME…UP!"

They said, "We can't pull you up. We ARE trying but the rope is stuck. You're going to have to do the best you can. You're going to have to just keep holding on."

"Guys I am tired. I've gone all this way. I am at the end of my rope literally and I don't know what to do."

"Hold on. Something is still making the rope stick." I thought "why don't you try to UNSTICK the stupid rope" but I couldn't waste the energy on spoken word.

"Just keep holding on. You can do it."

My hands started shaking. My body started shaking. I was beginning to get very scared. I didn't know what to do. Finally, my arms gave out and I fell!.... about seven or eight inches. The rope went to within five feet from the bottom of the cave. They knew it! I didn't. I had never been there before. Obviously they had. So, this was just a big trick for them. A joke on me, Ha. Ha…. A Bone & Cricket for me, and a Boone & Crockett for them, it was the trophy of their unintelligent lifetimes. They talked about it, and later about how they planned it.

Mercifully, they sent a light down, slowly descending casting beams of light in circular motions, eventually reaching my position on the cave floor. I was blind but now could see: Once in the darkness, now illuminated, I beheld a huge cave with a big beautiful room, not a never-ending pit. I also saw in the newly lit room a ladder made of rope which paralleled a wooden rung ladder that could be held onto for the climb up or down. "Out of the darkness into the light" came to mind.

The bible speaks volumes about dark and light. The meaning and consequences of darkness are as unmistakable as are the rewards of The Light. The Light called Jesus Christ is eternal and sent by the Father to send fleeing the darkness so all may see. What an amazing difference a little bit of light can make in a dark and cave-like life!

Had I known anything of details hidden by the darkness, the decent would have been easy, but that was not the point. The point was they wanted me to do exactly what I did. They knew what was happening and had planned it very specially for me. I got them back after that, each one little by little. I might accidentally butt burn one of them with the carbide lamp if they were in front of me and not moving "fast" enough, might tell them that the water was a little bit shallower than its true depth, or other things. Eventually, I got them all back, but that is just the way it happens, sooner or later it's quickly back to the bottom, having just ascended to the top of the heap. Reflecting back on an experience keeps it alive, often allowing the details to become some-what cloudy but the magnitude of the deeds growing propor-tionately to the telling of the saga. The Bone & Cricket predicament becomes the highlight of the trip.

You have heard me talk about my wife before and how I am continually amazed at the woman God gave me. I'm always trying to impress her, be the man of the mountain or strong guy, know-it-all in the woods, wilds, or wherever we are. I took her fishing on Cooper Creek when she was about 8 months pregnant with our first child, Lauren. Well, that might not be the smartest thing to do, but she was game for it, so we went tent camping and trout fishing. She loves camping and enjoys trout fishing with me. We had a great time sitting around the campfire anticipating the arrival of our new addition and the next days fishing, just the two us. We talked about how much fun fishing was, how the time just seemed to pass away, not thinking about schedules, and all the while being able to concentrate on enjoying each others company.

That night in camp after turning in for the day while hashing over the upcoming days fishing, we heard a raccoon noisily foraging through our stuff.

Therefore, I, being the "all-knowing frontiersman that I am" spoke, "Here's what we will do Susie (I hadn't started calling her mama yet). I'm not going to let that raccoon ransack our stuff. They're out here all the time, loafing all day scoping out what goodies can be stolen after the campers go to sleep. I know that's what he's doing. Not gonna happen tonight. Not here. No way! I'll show 'em. I am tougher and meaner than some lazy good for nothin' ole raccoon. I'm not going to let it have a free meal on us. No sir!

I'm going to unzip this tent real quiet like. The raccoon is just outside. I'm going to unzip and I want you to take this big flashlight and shine it in his beady little eyes, right in that burglar looking face when I open the tent. I'm going to scream at that menace and scare the heck out of him. That'll show him. I'm going to get him going so fast his stripes'll come off his tail. It will not want to mess with us ever again."

So I slightly unzipped the tent. Quietly, quietly, slowly, very slowly….Got right poised. Susie was aiming the light with precision accuracy in the direction of our lazy intruder, waiting only for my command to shine the million candle power death beam at our masked marauder. At that precise moment I realized the raccoon wasn't a raccoon.

Sitting two feet away staring face to face, eyeball to eyeball, was one of the biggest skunks I had ever seen chawing down on some snacks of bread and a few goodies we had been saving in a little sack. Not only did I NOT scream, I closed that tent quicker than you can imagine and in as manly a voice as I could muster whispered, "Do Not say a word. Do Not move a muscle. Don't even blink hard!

There is the biggest skunk out there I've ever seen, and it can have whatever it wants because if it sprays we will stink for months and it will be my fault."

So, I go from hero to zero, one more time, trying to impress the woman of my dreams. That seems to happen sometimes when we get puffed up in ourselves and forget who we really are and how incapable we can become.

I've spoken before about my buddy Wes, one of who I called "We the Three." We were always hanging out doing crazy things, hunting, fishing, or maybe accomplishing nothing more than tossing the football or shooting hoops. We richly enjoyed each others company and being outside. One particular evening we went to Clear Lake, a place his family owned not too far from where we lived. He was going to show me his new gun, a 357-magnum "Dirty Harry" pistol, to use deer hunting. He was always talking about how anyone could hunt with a rifle, but a real man, a real mountain man would hunt with a pistol. He bought this big deer shooting pistol and wanted me to see it. Enjoying guns, I thought I'd like that.

We sat on the back porch of this beautiful place and put a can down on the ground as a cheap target.

He said "Now this thing is pretty loud. You may want to cover your ears."

I said "Figgered it would be." And I did!

He continued with, "It's a big ole gun with a big ole payload. It's going to shoot hard."

With that, he shot and not only was it loud, but also easily noticed was the heat of the blast from the gun, as well as the concussion of sound from it. I was impressed. It was a big gun. So he shot it a time or two more, I shot it once, wasn't very close to the target but I figured, heck, as loud as it was the sound alone would knock something down or scare it to death if the missile sized projectile didn't hit it. He was all excited about that gun.

He said "You know, I believe I can shoot this can Dirty Harry style. Heck, it's not all that bad. It kicks some, but it's really not all that bad. I'm just going to shoot that target with one hand."

I wasn't sure who he was trying to convince me or him. Nonetheless, he put his arm out there one handing the gun, cocked it, squeezed the trigger and "BLAM," another sonic blast erupted from that magnum persuader, more resembling the shooting style of Dainty Mary instead of Dirty Harry.

He looked at me and I looked at him, both looking at that gun now upside down pointing directly back at him.

He had shot that gun one handed but the gun was bigger and a little bit badder than he was and had spun totally around in his hand. It was all he could do to keep it from dropping out of his hand onto the ground, hanging there by his finger pointing back at me and him, his grip totally wrenched asunder. I was impressed with Wes. He didn't curse, didn't say anything hardly at all except "Maybe I'll use two hands the next time." I had to agree with him. Two hands on that gun was a better choice.

He did take it hunting a couple of times and claims to have shot a deer with it once. Probably had about the same effect as I had on that can, just scared the dickens out of the deer and it ran off. He swore he thought he hit it, but I knew better. He always thought he had hit something, especially if no one was there to see it or knew a shot had been taken…. if you're by yourself it doesn't matter. If someone IS there you definitely have to have some proof about hitting the target instead of just shooting at it.

Of course, don't think either of us was always a Bone & Cricket or the Boone & Crockett guy, we both had our moments, I always enjoyed his mistakes.

I have to tell you a story about when he and I started turkey hunting. He really, really, really wanted to impress his uncle, Dr. Harvey Howell, who he called Uncle Harvey. I called him Dr. Harvey, a term of endearment a few people used with him. He was quite an exquisite outdoorsman himself. He was old school and knew all kinds of things about the outdoors, many being lost in time along with the teachers. When I think of a hunter or mountain man, an image of Dr. Harvey would be conjured up in my mind.

I've heard stories told by old friends sharing lifelong adventures, some accounts recollected by men of the wild, long in years and past their prime, but still holding a gleam in their eye and a multitude of expressions on their face, unfolding the stories of bygone years like the pages in a precious book. Accordingly, it would not have been uncommon for Dr. Harvey to hike for half a day up into the woods to go hunting in the Cohuttas or somewhere special, spend the night huddled around a little tiny fire, shoot a deer and carry it out, half one day, half the next. Other nearly unbelievable yarns of youthful days and great adventure held the listeners captive once the stories started flowing.

Therefore, Wes was always trying to impress Uncle Harvey. This time he was going to impress him and wanted me to be a part of it. During one of our hanging outs he said, "Let's go down and get some turkey calls. I've been with Uncle Harvey a couple of times turkey hunting and I believe I can do that. I'd really like to show him I can turkey hunt and could go by myself. He and Shep have been kinda showin' me and I could impress him going by myself and taking a turkey."

So we drove down to Athens to a gun shop to look at some guns since he was thinking about getting one anyway. It was always fun to get out and enjoy each other's company or have some fellowship doing things you like. He had read about or seen some calls that you put in your mouth.

"These will leave your hands free. You can stay very still as the ole Tom comes forward enticed by the sound of a big beautiful hen. It'll just take a little practice then "POW' a turkey to show Uncle Harvey."

There are lots of ways to call a turkey and his uncle

and cousins, Sam and Shep could really do a great job calling up a turkey. He wanted to do something a little bit different.

"There's a box call, a slate call, all manner of turkey calls," he said, "I believe I'm going to get one of those diaphragm calls.

You put 'em in your mouth and make some noise that sounds like a hen turkey clucking. I believe even you and of course, ESPECIALLY I could do that. You can make it sound far away or close to you, fast or slow, make different sounds and pitches." To reiterate his previous point: "You don't even have to move, so if a turkey is close and you're afraid it's going to see you, you can use this mouth call."

I thought that sounded good, had never done any turkey calling, but always wanted to. I had been with Wes a time or two turkey "hunting," (notice I said hunting) and since there needs to be turkeys for a legitimate hunt; not much finding, much less shooting, took place. One gobbler was heard a couple of times a long way off, but no meat was added to the freezer out of our early turkey hunting times…There were always two turkeys in the woods but they always both left in a truck.

We bought the mouth calls, spent the whole ride back and the rest of the day practicing with them, and unbelievably actually "looked" at the instructions, trimming the diaphragm to fit perfectly into the roof of our mouths. We would call on them and call to each other, pretending there were turkeys just around the next bend.

A few days later, it was time to show his Uncle Harvey the ability he had mastered calling turkeys, so I went with him. He clucked a time or two but Dr. Harvey did not seem too impressed. He clucked a time or two more with a little more animation, really cutting up with that turkey call and I thought he sounded pretty good. Knowing it was getting close to my turn. "I believe I can show him too" I thought. I wanted to go hunting and wanted him to see I'd been practicing too.

It never quite became my turn. After a while Dr. Harvey just kind of nodded his head like he did occasionally and said "Well boy, that sounds pretty good, but you've got the mouth call in backwards." Sure enough we'd had those things backwards, front to back. Instead of using our tongue on controlled forceful exhaling clucking on them, we were basically taking a long, slow, deep staccato breath through them.

Oops! Wes went from being a good turkey caller to a turkey himself. I was just glad I didn't get involved in it and show what a turkey I was to one of the great turkey hunters. I'm not sure Wes remembers some of the facts this way, but once again; it's my telling, not his.

I learned a lot that day. If you try to impress someone that is way better than you, you will have a more aBONE-dant life. Instead, you should watch listen and learn what they do. Sometimes we try to impress God "by showing" Him we can do it ourselves; by going, instead of watching where He is leading us, speaking instead of listening to what He's saying, and forgetting the history and lessons He's given us in His word and in our hearts and lives. It matters sometimes how you accomplish a task. Being able to do something right is better than just being able to do it.

Sometime after the mouth-calling escapade, Wes and

I were going turkey hunting near Adairsville close to where the pistol escapade took place. We knew some turkeys were there, at least one any way; while scouting the area (a new trick we learned) we had heard some gobbling, and seen scratching and tracks. That's all we needed: Just one. We had graduated, or I had graduated to a box call since I was too embarrassed to put the diaphragm call back in my mouth. Wes decided that the box call was pretty good too, maybe for the same reason.

We went hunting and we (Wes) decided that since I hadn't been much with Dr. Harvey, had only been with Wes a time or two, and even though I had practiced, Wes would do the calling.

Besides, "When you hit a bad note on that call it will sound horrible. We don't want to scare off maybe the only turkey here. We need our best chance at this one."

So, Wes would do the calling, and I'd sit quietly. We'd separate apart a little bit just like Wes had learned and I had seen on T.V.

Our plan was simple. Go there and if there weren't any turkeys, we would try another place close to where I live. Dr. Harvey owned and allowed us to hunt several big tracts of land close to my house. His car was very often parked along the road outside the gate. He would NEVER drive in to hunt. "That's why God gave us legs."
He said we could hunt there, but we knew it really was one of his favorite places to turkey hunt. We hated to go over there kill all his turkeys, so even with permission, our initial hunt would be somewhere different, and our default destination, not that we needed one; would be there.
So we went over near Adairsville and hunted in the morning not really hearing or seeing anything except a bunch of squirrels on their lifes' mission: Irritate every hunter who enters the woods during deer or turkey season. Hide never to be seen during squirrel season.

We got back close to the car and Wes said, "You know it's different when you do a call out in the woods versus in your house or on your porch. It just sounds different. Really you just need to practice how it sounds, your tone, getting to hear it, and maybe just working the call a little bit, so why don't you call a few times. We've got nothing to lose. There are no turkeys out here it seems today anyway. We didn't hear anything and we're close to the car, so just call a few times."

I said, "That's a great idea! I'm glad you said that. Glad I have that opportunity, so let's stop here." I surmised optimistically "Never would have gotten the chance if we had heard some turkeys…. Aren't we lucky?"

I called a few notes on that box and as I quit calling a cow bellowed "mooooo". Straight-faced and still intently focused on the hunt at first, then simultaneously refocused on the turn of events, both just died laughing. We thought that was the funniest thing we'd ever heard, so he started calling me "Cow Boy", "Cow Caller," which is sort of appropriate since the only call I made had been answered by a cow. Unheard of until that precise moment, I believe it is a term of extreme honor rarely bestowed.

Since we doubted it was cow season, we left that place and decided to finish the hunt, spending a little bit of time close to Holly Springs. We got out and started walking into the woods, using the same method as before. Wes was going to call some…Listen… Walk a little bit… Call… Listen….Walk a little bit… Call… Listen… Walk a little bit.

We knew more or less, where they were and where they had been since Dr. Harvey told us they had been there and would always be in the general vicinity. With turkeys, exact location is not as important as hunting deer, duck, or squirrel. You can hear a gobbler for a quarter mile or so, so we went to where we had been instructed. Our default destination was a destination of de fault this morning: Maybe we were too late or they had gone up on the mountain, or become shut mouth. We didn't get into any turkeys at that spot either. So, same way back out of the woods, just in case we'd call… Listen… Walk a little bit... Call… Listen… Walk a little bit.

Close to the car I said "Let me try it again."

Earlier that morning was moooving, not the outcome expected, but I knew with each attempt I would get a little more confident, feel a little better about myself allowing my calling prowess to improve.

"I think I can do a better job this time. Let's see how it sounds."

So I hit about 4 or 5 notes on that box. They sounded really, really good this time. As soon as I finished.... "moooo".... a cow from nowhere!

I lived near there, no cows were anywhere close, and that's a fact! But that cow on the other side of the mountain, other side of the river, other side of the universe, somewhere, somehow, heard that call. Just like his buddy, this hearing impaired, low IQ even for a bovine, thought the call sounded like a cow. That was unbelievably ridiculous! We laughed, and laughed. I never struck a note again that season. We didn't get to go a lot, but when we did I never even picked up my call. It was a long time before I had the guts to try it again. It was just too funny and I couldn't concentrate on what I was doing for thinking about the time I called two cows in the same day, in two different places, with the same call.

I've learned several things from hanging out, listening to, and being with my best buddy Joshua, my son. He taught me a lot of things without the benefit of age or experience. Early on, we were hunting squirrels one afternoon and had shot two or three just out back of the house. Sitting there really quiet, he leaned over and said "Dad, I see a squirrel."

"Well, shoot it son."

"But, no Dad I see a squirrel….."

Interrupting him, "Well, son do you have a shot?"

"Yes, Dad but…"

Again hearing but not listening… "Well, if you can shoot it then go ahead and shoot it."

I was more concerned with just shooting the squirrel and getting the task completed, neither paying attention, nor listening; not hearing what he had to say, or even watching what he was doing, than enjoying the time with him.

So he sat right there and said, "Ok, dad, I'll do it!

He shot.

"Son, did you hit the squirrel?"

"Yes, I did daddy," was his reply.

"Well, let's go get it."

We stood up and about fifteen feet, the distance from the end of the barrel of his 20-gage shotgun, lay a tail; no meat just a tail, all that was left of the sum of the parts now scattered imperceptible.

He said "Dad, I tried to tell you the squirrel was just RIGHT there. I thought it was too close."

"Well son, you were right. I should have listened to you."

When we get caught up in not paying attention, are too "into the moment" not listening to family and friends, or concentrating on what we're doing, thinking we know more than they do or what's being said is not important enough for us to take pause to hear; precious time and fellowship are lost.

Four not quite as close

Another time, Joshua and I were fishing on the Hiawassee in Tennessee. With a guide procured for the trip we could fish a lot and not worry about wading from shoal to shoal or taking care of the boat. It was really hot, one June afternoon. I was at the front of the boat, he at the back. I was really, really, really trying to catch some fish; determined, flailing the water, slinging the line, casting my arm off, trying to catch just one. I could only think of four reasons for a fishing trip: "Catch fish, catch fish, catch fish, and catch fish".... I was doing my part... fishing, fishing, and more fishing.

I looked back and Joshua was leaning back at the rear of the boat with his shoes off and his feet in the water. I was furious!!

I thought," Here we are. I paid a lot of money for a one day float trip just so I can enjoy spending time with Joshua."

(We always tried to do something special together every year, usually a week at a time when possible).

"This was time we have to spend together and he's not even fishing."

Being upset, I looked back at him and said, "Joshua, what are you doing!!?"

Never looking up hands behind his head came the reply "Dad, I'm enjoying the day. Having a great time, thanks for bringing me! What about you? Catching any fish?"

Then it hit me. It never is about CATCHING the fish, not about maniacally casting the line. The important part is always about the JOURNEY, not just getting out and catching something or shooting something, but the entire trip, each day, the fellowship ….

I started relaxing. I put my fly rod down for a bit.

He said "I've been watching this fish hawk a while and he's catching more fish than you!!"

I thought, "How true that is!!!"

But, I learned a valuable lesson from my son that day. Our focus should not be on the end result or the target, but the spotlight should be on what is going on while we are getting there. Just like life.

Another time fishing took me back to that great place in north Georgia on a secluded area of Jacks River. The good fishing requires a long walk and even then it's a struggle, you may not catch a single one of the native trout especially if the water is clear or low, even for the experts like some of my buddies think they are. The first time fishing there I never got a fish, but a couple more times paid off in numbers of strikes, the more times there, the better I got. It was always fun, but as I got better so did the fishing, and it's always more fun to catch a fish than not! An eight inch fish was a good fish on that river, but I have caught some big fish there as well. One I've already talked about was that nice seventeen inch brown trout. Jacks River has fish in it, whether you could catch them or not could be problematic, but not the point, it is a beautiful place to go.

Ted Perry and I decided one evening we would go after work and wet a fly or two until dark then come on home. Jacks River is about two hours from where I live, so it was not a big deal in the summer especially when we didn't have to get up early the next day for work. "We took off, went on up there, and took to fishin'." About the time it was getting dark, we decided to get off the river and walk back on one of the old trails along the river made from a narrow gauge rail left while harvesting the wood there years, and years ago. Many of the trails, once rails avoid the steepest terrain and run along the natural course of the river following its moderate grade as it meanders along the ridges and valleys. We started walking back and the lightning bugs just "came alive." By the thousands, they were everywhere flashing their neon advertisements to light our way, the most spectacular display we had ever seen.

Once at the car it would be forty five minutes to an hour back to paved "civilization," the McDonald's on Hwy. 76. Starting back on this old dirt road the lights on the car went out, efforts to remedy the dilemma were all futile, we thought "Oh my goodness, what is going on here? The lights are NOT coming back on." There was only one option: go dark and slowly… go very… very…. slowly.

Then a thought came up: "We've got a flashlight!" Ted was driving so I rolled down the window leaning way out deftly pointing toward our goal: stay on the road and out of the ditches; and held the flashlight out of the car. We crept at a snails pace ever so slowly forward down that old dirt road following the forward facing glow. Getting to Highway 5, a paved road, made it some better. It was not nearly as winding, but forced by the dark, the light slowly dimming, we continued creeping along with the flashlight in front of the car leading us toward our destination of hope for help.

Well, I'm sure if you saw us you would think. "What are them two rednecks doin'? Them good ole boys don't got no lights on their car and thera usin' a flashlight to guide themselves home. Been out drinkin,' 'probly"

We eventually got to McDonald's some time later, much later than planned, and had planned on being home way before that. It was probably around 11 o'clock I guess, overwhelmed with relief upon seeing the Golden Arches, our "Evereadys" no longer so ready, and the prospect of calling for rescue, neither had looked at a clock. The sequence of events were playing out before anyone had cell phones; as a matter of fact, I doubt ANY phones were standard issue where we'd been, so obviously we didn't have a car phone cell phone or bat phone. ET could not even help us!

We used the pay phone at McDonald's and Ted called home, told them where we were, what had happened, and "come and get us," finally allowing our arrival home after two in the morning. The only problem was in our haste we had forgotten to call my wife, Susie, and tell her what was happening. By the time of our appearance she had called everyone she could think of including the police. She knew that my brother-in-law, Scott, would know where we were fishing (he had been "schooled some" on this part of the river before), and where our mutilated or dismembered bodies could be found. She thought the worst thing had happened to us. Of course, it hadn't….We both caught some fish.

The tale was told over and over again. The time we spent on the trip was way shorter than the time spent telling about it. The more we told it, the darker the night became, the longer the road continued, the bigger the tale grew.

A couple years later, my brother-in-law Scott and I again went up to the same place on the Jacks, turning left on Hwy 5 is where our no light late night McDonald's stands. Scott had heard the story so we stopped for breakfast. Having to get up really early, to be parked before day-break and be able to finish our hike in and start fishing at first light of the morning, often casting before the fog was burned off by the rising sun, always made two good ole boys hungry. We drove up to the drive-thru and ordered.

From the speaker came, "We're out of bread."

"What do you mean you're out of bread?"

She said, "You can have your Egg McMuffins but there are no muffins. We don't have any."

We thought, this is a crazy thing, but "we'll take those muffins without bread" because we needed something to sustain us for the day. We went on and fished and had a great day, even caught a few.

On the way back the discussion came to "Well, we should give them a second chance. Let's stop by that McDonald's." It was on in the afternoon about 2:00 and we hadn't eaten anything except those Egg McMuffins… without muffins.

Now Scott and I are pretty big guys with big engines and big engines need a lot of energy. We had worked pretty hard that morning. A good hike to the river, fighting the water, and a longer hike back burns a lot of fuel. Man, we were ready right then and there for a Big Mac, some fries, and to get the dust out of our throats from that now twice traveled old gravel road. That "great ole big Coke" we had salivated about on the hour or so hike from the river to get to the car, then the other forty five minutes to get to McDonald's was paramount to the day. We were REALLY ready for a Mac Attack.

So, we got to the window and said, "We'd like two large fries, two large cokes and four big Macs"

Almost immediately the girl said "Didn't ya'll come by this morning?"

"Yes ma'am we sure did."

"I thought I remembered y'all and that truck….We don't have any meat!"

"You don't have any meat?!?"

"No sir. We finally got the muffins, but we ran out of meat.

We got fries!! We don't have any meat."

"Well, I guess fries and a Coke will have to do."

Ever since then my brother-in-law Scott has not liked McDonald's. Susie and I take Caleb, his son to McDonald's on Saturdays. Scott does not go. Occasionally he will get a breakfast if we are out and it's all that is available, but mostly he will not get any of their so-called lunch or dinner items.

Sometimes, we have one thing we stand for or that we do very well. If God gives you talent and you do not use it, or the value of your reputation is based on a product and you do not have what has been advertised, all you can do is provide a substitute: you are not worth much.

Therefore, when God gives us a talent or ability and we do not use it, we are just like a McDonald's without muffins or meat.

Another food item food time was again with my brother-in-law Scott in attendance. Do you see a pattern here? Scott likes to eat. If you saw him you'd know it, as previously stated: he's a big ole boy, in good shape, but he's a big boy. I like to eat too, and whenever we get to go somewhere, hunting, fishing, scuba diving or something else, we enjoy trying different palate pleasers by sampling the local eateries. Scott's corollary "If the locals eat there it's usually different and good." Sometimes all that is available are chain restaurants, but if you can find out from the regulars where they like to eat, then the cuisine is usually pretty decent. We were at Panama City Beach doing our check out certification dive (prior to Dons' influence on our diving); staying at a place called Spy Glass Inn, which I am sure, was the only place on the beach at the time without a beach view, wedged between two hotels, a little triangle of a building. No phone except the one in the lobby, no air conditioning; well sorta' kinda' worked I guess anyway, blowing some hot Panama City Beach ocean air, comprised the sum total of the amenities. It was the only hotel that you could see nothing but buildings in any direction. These accommodations were typical for us on one of our "adventures". I'm sure Don King must have made our reservations.

We asked, "Where is a good place to eat." They gave us the name of this little diner place, the kind with a wrap around counter like an old 50's restaurant. It was early morning, breakfast time, and we were ready for some good home cooked food. We had worked hard the day before diving. If you are not very good at diving, especially when first learning, you use a lot of energy trying to get things accomplished; that was us, so we were ready for that breakfast. Scott ordered some food and chocolate milk, and I ordered my regular stuff.

He said, "Try this chocolate milk."

So, I took a nice big swig, and about the time I had a large quantity down my throat…"Is that spoiled?"

Of course it was! And of course I began to spew the milk back out of my mouth as he gently said "I thought so."

Milk is one thing, Chocolate milk another, spoiled, it takes on a category all its own. If you have never had spoiled chocolate milk you need to try that at least once in you lifetime, you will never forget it, and you will never forgive the person who did it to you or for you; however you wish to look at it.

I got Scott back or rather Scott got Scott back. That's the way it works: Boone and Crockett to Bone and Cricket; hero to zero. Although I had nothing to do with it, I did enjoy it. I'm not saying he deserved it but I'm not saying he didn't, there's no use crying over spoiled milk.

One fall six or eight years ago, Scott and his boys were raking leaves at Grandmama and Granddaddy's house, a great service for them, and the boys had a good time doing it. There was no shortage of old oaks with leaves covering the ground layer upon layer; raking them into a monstrous pile and depositing them in the big ditch that ran in front of the house required an all day job. As a bonus, the boys were jumping in the man made mega pile having a great time, and were just about through scraping up and collecting the remnant summer greens turned brown as the last load was being gathered up. They put them in the back of Scott's truck in a big tarp, drove them to the ditch, and pulled them off the pick-up, adding volume to the ever-increasing mountain of leaves.

Scott's truck was there, a key component in the story. He had a big Dodge truck. It was really jacked up, big tires, loud pipes etc... You know the type....a rather redneckish "Georgia country boy" truck, notwithstanding, it was a nice truck I must say.

I was not there, but according to reliable first hand account witnesses this was how the incident unfolded:

Standing up in that big jacked up truck; he had seen his boys diving into the leaves and figured he could show them a thing or two. Beholding the pile of leaves, he then confidently proclaimed "Huh! Watch this. This is how a real man does it," took a big leap and did a swan dive into the pile of leaves. The problem was he misjudged the distance, didn't hit a leaf at all, went slap over the whole pile and landed shoulder first, onto the ground. I already told you Scott's a big ole boy and a big ole boy flying through the air from a jacked up truck onto the ground is not a very pretty sight, comical, yes, but not pretty. Well, he realized the second he hit, something was wrong. Lying there face first like a spent projectile on the ground, shoulder badly dislocated… he could not get up. With leaf dust all around him, choking, spitting, and spewing, with all his might, again, he tried… again, he could not get up.

The boys were lifting, trying…face first, flat prone, he stayed. Soon Sharon thought she was going to have to get Granddaddy's tractor to get him off the ground and into the truck. He finally pulled himself around onto his side and with as much strength as could be mustered from he and family minus Granddaddy's tractor managed to sit up awkwardly, in some serious pain. Big boy or not, he was hurting and if you looked at his arm hanging three or four inches lower than the other, you would have thought, "OH….MY…GOODNESS! That is terrible!"

So, they got him into the truck and to the emergency room. All the way there Sharon just could not help laughing. She'd look at Scott and he'd be moaning and she'd giggle, then laugh, then back straight faced; after a bit she'd giggle, then laugh and composing herself manage another straight face. She kept saying "I'm sorry Scott, it's just funny!"

Finally, Scott got to the emergency room and they took his history with a brief description of the events as they transpired. He had had on his camo stuff, which he wore while working, and somebody said, "Oh man, did you fall out of a tree stand?"

"No… I was raking and jumped into a pile of leaves."

They were shocked at that. After a few of the same sort of questions from emergency room "citizens" and staff and his honest to life answers he got to thinking. "I don't think I should have told that."

That is NOT a good story to have to admit to, you know, this big ole guy in camo during hunting season and all he had for a story was "jumping into a pile of leaves from the back of a mile high pickup."

"A pile of leaves…?"

"Seriously…?"

"Jumping, you say…?"

"Really?"

Three or four more people were kind enough to show him their concern with questions. Embarrassment became prevalent with each truthful admission answering his predicament.

Another asked him "Did you fall out of a tree stand?"

He finally said "Yep, I sure did" and went on with that lie for the remainder of his ER visit. Somehow, the truth just wasn't believable and far too traumatizing to tell.

They took him to x-ray for confirmation of the damage done by the Olympic style swan dive. To obtain multiple views aiding in the diagnosis and course of treatment the sweet little radiology tech said, "Mr. Mauldin, I'm going to have to move your arm to a different position."

His reply short and to the point was, "If you do, I'm going to bust you in the mouth!"

Well, by the time I got to the hospital and gave a little anesthesia to the leaf jumper, his attitude was miraculously changed. He was now loving everybody he came in contact with including the x-ray tech who minutes before was going to need dentures if she took one step closer to him. Dr. Brunette was able to put his shoulder back in place and we brought him home. The sequence of events planted the seed in my mind for Scott's Christmas present that year. He received nicely framed, much like a stained glass window suitable for display, a copy of his x-ray. Attached was a cartoon clip picture of a little old man swan diving from the back of a ratty pickup into a pile of leaves. The caption read "Huh. Watch this. This is how a real man does it." A Boone for a Bone!

A couple years later he went back to the doctor's office with a shoulder injury unrelated to the leaf pile but they brought up that incident anyway. It is, as you know, part of his permanent medical record!

Scott told them "I'm not telling anybody that story. I don't want anybody to know it. As a matter of fact, that conjures up bad memories for me, so just erase it from my chart if you can."

So, Jay Brunette, an orthopedic surgeon, the one who reduced his shoulder originally, and by the way just happens to be a good friend of ours, divulged the story as it had been told before stopping only briefly to laugh. It was especially sweet to the ones who knew Scott, knew how embarrassing it was for him, and what a golden Boone and Crockett moment it was for the rest of us.

My daughter Lauren is another unbelievable Boone and Crockett gift from God in my life. She grew up hiking and camping whether she liked it or not.... Eventually she liked it. No one is immune to the opportunity for a Bone and Cricket moment. Eventually one will creep up on you while unaware you are minding your own business peacefully admiring the wonders of God's creation. For her the time had come, a unique moment. None of her friends and very few people have ever experienced it. We were part of it and give first-hand testimony retelling it as only bystanders and onlookers can.

For Susie and my 20th anniversary, our family took a trip to Africa celebrating the blessings and joy God had given us as a family. I could let you contemplate how awesome a place Africa is and what a Boone and Crockett time we must have experienced. Both are correct, but with explanations. There is no way to truly express the experience or location of Africa. As one person said, "It's big enough to be a continent." Africa is a hugely vast land with a multitude of people and extremely diverse landscapes.

The part of Africa we visited was Tanzania, a country of east central Africa, the land made famous as the cradle of civilization by the "discoveries" in the Olduvi Gorge by Dr. Leakey in the early part of the 20th century, the land of The Serengeti, Ngorongoro Crater, Maasai, and the big five: Elephants, Lions, Rhino, Water Buffalo, and Hippo. The sights, sounds, smells, people, vistas, and animals are all beyond words. Reading about Africa in a thousand books could not replace being there for one day.

There are not enough pictures to represent the single vision over-looking a seemingly endless expanse, full of multitudes of animals, turning into tiny silhouette specks in the distance as the landscape vanishes like vapor into the horizon. The story is not so much about the place Africa, but a single pause in the journey and a Bone and Cricket moment for Lauren, creating a Boone and Crockett for the rest of us that reanimates the trip and brings bright memories to the forefront of our minds.

Lauren did NOT want to go to Africa. "Too many bugs, spiders, bugs, snakes, bugs, and bugs….We are going to stay in a tented camp instead of a hotel, AND WE CHOSE the tented camp?... Outdoor toilets?" were some of her strongly voiced concerns. It is ironic that it was Lauren with the first "spot" of the trip. While riding in an open top Landcruiser, Lauren shouted, "There goes a Zebra"! We laughed. In her excitement and haste she couldn't even get the words to match her thoughts. Standing not fifty yards away was a giraffe. And no it wasn't striped.

That small blunder made good fun throughout the trip. We would kid about seeing "this or that" often wrongly mocking Lauren's first sighting or "spot" as the guides would call them. The zebra/giraffe incident is not her most infamous, best told, or most beloved moment, however.

A different day we had been on a wildlife drive and had seen many critters including lions, elephants, hippos and scores of herd animals, some within feet of the vehicle. We stopped under one huge tree to watch a large troupe of baboons.

Lauren had taken the seat on the very back of the vehicle unencumbered by the cover of the roof, busily watching the interactions of babies and mothers and some of the adolescent and older baboons as well. I thought it closely resembled some of the family reunions I've been to, but I'm not going to say which side of the family.

Lauren remarked "Oops! I better get back under the top, it's starting to rain," an odd statement since it was one of those perfect African skies we had grown accustomed to and adored; bright blue and barren of clouds as far as the eye could see. There was however, sitting in the tree just a few feet above my "new found love for Africa" daughter, a big male baboon purposefully "raining" on Lauren's head, the same "bug girl" who didn't' want to go to Africa. I was glad she had not known about male baboon territorial defenses or bathroom habits. The look on her face when the realization of what had just taken place was as the saying goes… Priceless! Boone for us. Bone, definitely Bone for her. I've never met anyone who can share a Bone and Cricket/Boone and Crockett moment quite like that one.

Several years later in spite of her close encounter of the baboon kind, Lauren rates her time in Africa very high on the list of her most favorite memories growing up. She really did love her time there and the tent camp was awesome, besides "there weren't all that many bugs, anyway." She was the first one excitedly jumping at the chance to use the shower tent and the first one to say how cool it was for her there.

Even so, it was a pleasant surprise when she said her fondest memory growing up was the times we spend every year camping as a family for Thanksgiving. Time spent with family, not some big trip was her Boone and Crockett favorite memory of a lifetime. I'll have to say ditto to that.

I would be remiss if I didn't tell another Boone and Crockett story involving my precious gift from God, Lauren. One year when she was twenty, Susie and I bought her a pair of waders and a fly rod for her birthday in anticipation of visiting Joshua in Yellowstone that year while he was a summer missionary. She was soooo excited that she got that for her present! I was shocked. I thought she was kidding but she wasn't. While there, I had the privilege of teaching Lauren some of the finer points of fly fishing. My beautiful wife Susie was also fishing so it was my honor to act as their guide.

I'll tell you, there's just something breathtaking about seeing two beautiful ladies in waders and camo, fly fishing the Firehole River in Yellowstone National Park.

Since Susie was about seventy-five yards upstream from Lauren, going back and forth between the two lovelies was easy and very enjoyable for me. While helping Susie one particular time I heard a scream coming from Lauren's place on the river and thought "Oh my! What the dickens was that?!"

Quickly the sound reverberated again and fearing the worst I immediately looked to see if a grizzly, wolf, bison, or Bigfoot was near my daughter, then heard it again, but this time while looking at her. It was not any of my fears manifest, but Lauren shouting "WOOOHOO." She had cast to; hooked, and was now working toward her very excited hands, a native Yellowstone Cutthroat trout. How cool is that? A Boone all the way!!!!

CHAPTER FOUR
The Outfitter and Guide

Earlier this year a friend of mine, Eric Webster, and I were going deer hunting. Now Eric had "never been deer hunting before," "always wanted to go so this would be my first time." ("Never done somethin' before 'til I done it for the first time" is a common saying used where I come from.)

Consequently, I said "Well, Eric come on I've got some stands that I built, actually blinds, that you can sit in. You don't have to climb a tree, they are very nice, a city boy like yourself will be just fine in them."

The words spoken to Eric brought from deep within memories about the first few times that I was really, really excited about hunting or fishing. In those early days, like Eric, I was green as a pickle and had no idea what to expect, so I instructed him:

"Here's what you'll need... A license, of course...You need to wear camo, although that's not real important because we will be hunting out of the blind... orange is necessary coming to and from the woods. Not just regular orange, but three hundred square inches of hunter orange worn from the waist up. I have a vest... No, you don't have to measure it... You need to take something that is warm since sitting still can get kind of cold, a flashlight because we will be going in the dark. Then anything else you personally require will be fine, but basically we're going to be sitting there waiting for the deer enjoying nature's display masterfully laid out before us."

I thought, "that's how an outfitter talks," just like the one instructing when my wife, Ted Perry, and his wife walked into a fly shop in West Yellowstone on the very first trip to Yellowstone. I had fly fished some, although it was not something I considered myself to be very good at back then, (reminds me of Scott) and although I had practiced and could fish a little bit, I had never fished or been anywhere like Yellowstone. Oh my goodness! Everything along the journey and upon reaching that marvelous place, every step, every turn was something unusual… something different…something fantastic.

We stepped into a fly fishing/outfitter shop called Blue Ribbon Flies. Figuring we were Blue Ribbon kinda' guys, why not go to Blue Ribbon Flies? We made a great choice and later learned that Blue Ribbon Flies is owned and operated by the world's leading authority on fishing the Yellowstone. Craig Mathews and his wife are incredible folks with a love for such an awe-inspiring place and the people that visited it.

We started asking the folks "What do we need?" They knew exactly where to go, where the fish were, and what and where the fish would be biting. Because the park is so large there may be good fishing on one end but not the other, or might be raining at one place and not another, and maybe a fire burning somewhere else. Knowing where to go and what flies to use would be paramount in successfully fishing "new territory." The ones at the shop knew the conditions of the water, numbers of fish, and the hatch they were after, as well as everything about the rivers, creeks, and lakes, and much about the entire the park. They gave us a list of things we needed: waders, a certain weight fly rod, flies, line and leader, sunscreen, sunglasses, bug spray, layers of clothing for temperature changes, and rain gear. Some of this, of course, we purchased long before in anticipation of the journey. We were not fully prepared for all we planned to do, or everything we saw, and even though we equipped ourselves using the information we had, it was insufficient to fully reach our goal. They continued giving us advice to complete our desired task based on where we were going, how to get there, and what would be needed upon arrival.

I was doing the same with Eric, thinking the similarities interesting. When you are going on a journey, especially somewhere you "haven't been before until the very first time," directions are required, and prior to departure, you should gather as much information as possible about it in preparation.

Eric's pre-hunt knowledge so far was limited to the data pieced together based on TV, books, or what others had said. At this point he knew:

He was going to meet me at my house or somewhere along the way.

I would drive.

It would be dark, so a light would be necessary going to the blind.

We would head out through the woods.

I would get him to the right place…he hoped!

He was on the journey for the first time.

He had an idea where we were going and the end point. That was about it.

In the journey of life, we need an outfitter, just like Yellowstone. It wouldn't have done any good to go there and only listen to those guys say: "You need waders and a jacket. Dress in layers because it is cold in the morning and hot in the afternoon. You need different types of flies…these are the ones they're after in the morning, these are for the afternoon. If you don't go to Slough Creek you'll want a different fly and you'll want different tackle, either sinking tip or floating."

To be successful, action would have to be implemented based on whatever guidance they had given. It would be paramount in fulfilling my desire to successfully fish those great waters, without it I'd be lost. I could disregard the advisement given and still go out, get in the water, and flail about, perchance even catch a few, but the greater reward comes from doing something right and is far more satisfying than simply doing it. The guide helps implement the good counsel given, as he instructs how to use the information and equipment provided by the outfitter throughout the journey, especially as the circumstances change.

Guides are interesting creatures. Some are Boone and Crockett worthy, very enjoyable with vast knowledge base and are invaluable mentors while traveling with them. Others I've met ashamedly have not even advanced to the grade of dog Bone or baby Cricket. The latter need mentioning for enlightenment. When choosing a guide, Elmer Fudd, the great cartoon philosopher, would caution….."Be vewy, vewy careful"…..Sound advice from one who sometimes couldn't tell duck season fwom wabbit season! One day on the water or in the woods with a bad guide is one wasted day. Following the wrong guide in life is devastating!

While fishing the Santee-Cooper for giant catfish with some friends one morning, we awoke to a ground clinging, wet feeling, thick as mud, fog cloud. The guide assured us there would be no problem fishing since early morning low visibility was a common occurrence, he knew the lake very well and had a GPS, a Global Positioning

System. Once boarded and gear stowed, we headed slowly away from the dock toward the open water of the channel.

The Santee Cooper is a huge shallow lake created at the beginning of WWII from a cypress forest to generate power for the war effort. The government was in such a hurry to flood the lake that many of the trees were left standing and most of the stumps still remain.

Navigating the stump-filled channels requires vigilance and patience. Some of our crew, on the lookout for stray trees or stumps, was at the bow of the boat while puttering at snail's pace in the fog worthy of a horror show. Eagle eye observation was needed as well while on the lookout for the tell tale point of land signaling the open water and the commencement of fishing.

After about forty-five minutes successfully traveling stump free, excitement filled the still fog-filled air. Thanks to near perfect watchdog vision from the sentries at the front of the boat, something was becoming visible, though barely. "It has to be the point of land." We were, after all, following the GPS, and our guide, noticing the goal we were seeking, began steering with increased vigor toward our first spot of the day.

Lights, dimly at first, then brightening, in a long row were also being observed as we got closer and closer. This was quite puzzling to the guide. He knew the point of land being searched for had a navigation light, though usually much brighter placed at the end of it, and it was a single light, not several in a row.

Thirty seconds later, wild exclamations from the "enlightened ones" in the front along with their rapid retreating toward the back of the boat, echoed in the early morning stillness.

"Look out! Look out! It's a dock! The dock! We're headed right for it! Go left! Turn left!"

We thought the guide knew how to use his fancy, state of the art hundred way point GPS... So did he!

Fortunately, the boat in a reverse sliding, bottom scraping, full throttle, sand-spewing stop, came to rest just shy of the dock, our original starting and planned ending point. We just thought we would get to do a little fishing before winding up back there.

Sometimes we need a GPS, or map. But, just like the boat, having a GPS and not using it, will do no good. In a car, the GPS might say, "Make a legal u-turn at the next appropriate place." "Make a legal u-turn..." When off the "chosen" trail it even tells how to go back to the point where IT knows where you are.

Without guidance, which path do you take? Here? There? Occasionally you can get back to the main trail, but time is wasted purposelessly. A GPS or map uses satellite adjusted bearings or a compass, a standard with which every piece of information is derived from and points back to. It's the origin, fixed unmoving and unchanging point, giving direction for which way to go. If you turn the map upside down and try to follow it you will never get to the right place, you will be going in the wrong direction. Therefore, you need a map, and compass or bearing, from a known unwavering point to get started in the right direction in order to complete your journey to the point you were seeking. In life, there is a GPS, standing for God Provided Salvation, and Jesus Christ is His name.

Wes and I were scouting our deer hunting area on Hanging Mountain, when we came upon some glow in the dark pins stuck into trees marking someone's trail to and from a deer stand. We figured if some city slicker (obviously) needed help finding his way in the dark, he probably didn't need to be hunting in our territory. We were concerned that someone so feeble might get hurt way out in the woods. Besides, the markers were going similarly in the direction we hunted. Always the considerate teacher, we gave them the opportunity to learn a little more about hunting in the wilds by moving the reflectors; that once followed, would lead in a circle.

If an outfitter says "take this map wear your stuff walk five miles and take the second left," and you do everything except you "keep to the right" as Wes once counseled, you might end up on the right river but at the wrong place, hitting the periphery of the target but missing the bulls eye. You have to follow the guidance CAREFULLY! It keeps you going in the right direction. God gave us His word as a map. We have to follow his word just as the outfitter gives us a map of the area and says, "This is the best place to fish… for the best hunting, go there…here is a short-cut…but avoid this place."

The dangers in Yellowstone parallel lifes' snares and pitfalls, area specific advice is very important. There are places you do not want to wander through or go near; super heated thermals and geysers hot enough to parboil

the flesh from your bones, cliffs hidden from sight, easily fallen off, deceivingly deep or swift water ready to sweep away.

The accessories listed by the outfitter given to go with the journey must be put together in the order they are needed, based on a particular quest and destination. If some- one were to go fishing in Yellowstone full as a tick with equipment, the whole kit and caboodle; waders, jacket, fly rod, and all the paraphernalia listed by the outfitter and nothing of it are used, or the waders are placed on arms, and the jacket on feet what good does that do? Just because they have the equipment does not mean they are going to be using it correctly. Different parts of the journey require different pieces of the provisions given by the outfitter. Is the equip- ment suitable? Try fly fishing using a salt-water rig with a 5-pound weight on the end of it. The presentation of the fly, although resembling several fishing friends, would lack finesse and would not work. Take a fly rod to a skeet shoot? That's not going to bust many skeet. All the finest equipment in the world is useless if it is not used for the purpose it was intended. Even with our stuff on appropriately and we are ready to hunt, fish, or take the next step in life, we still have to follow the map and directions and take the first step and each subsequent step thereafter.

When I'm with a guide, or I am the guide, sound recommendations should be given based on experience and knowledge, sometimes it seems, that that advice is ridicu- lous.

One such lesson came from a guide on our first trip to the record holding trout fishing destination White River in

Arkansas. My brother in law Scott set up the trip and guide. During one day spin fishing with red wigglers we ran out of bait, a cardinal sin for a guide and automatic suspension of any anticipated tip. I was in the front of the boat and when the guide realized our predicament reached under his seat causing my thought.   "Good. More bait. Still gets a tip!"

I expected the guide to have what we needed, hooks, rods, reels, boat, AND bait, since it was all included "for the price of admission." What I did NOT expect was the guide to pull out a bag of tiny marshmallows, not the kind you roast over the campfire, mind you, but the ones you might add to a good cup of freshly made hot chocolate. Scott was less impressed but more shocked. He still had a one remaining worm on his hook, which he quickly lost, and a couple pieces he found in the bottom of his container in the bottom of the boat, which he was unwilling to share. He was "not going to use no stinkin' marshmallows to catch no stinkin'trout. I drove eleven hours and a whole bunch of miles and I ain't gonna use no stinkin' marshmallows."

I had no choice. I was out of bait and Scott obviously wasn't going to share. He had his knife out and open on the seat beside him. He said it was to cut the worms into as little pieces as possible, but I was not going to test him on it.

I reluctantly put on a mellow mallow and cast, evidently with perfect precision to a junk food junkie trout. A nice rainbow was in the boat as Scott pierced and pieced together the last of his slimy friends onto his hook. Another marshmallow trout was landed in much the same manner as before, as the flimsy pieces of the last repast were stolen from "worm Scrooge's" hook. Being unable to withstand it any longer, forced baitless, Scott humbly asked for "some of them marshmellas." We caught a LOT of fish. Reluctantly, even though Scott still detested marshmallows, thought the guide did a good job and deserved a tip. We later discovered a long held world record trout had been caught in that river from the end of a dock on corn….and a marshmallow. Rumor had it our unimpressive guide held a striking resemblance to that angler.

Even following the map using a compass, doing what you think is right, the guide might adjust your course or instruct you to do something different than YOU had anticipated, like our White River marshmallow fishing connoisseur.

If the guide says "Well, today boys they're not bitin' here," fishing there is still an option, but the likelihood of catching some is slim and the time would be wasted and unproductive. There was a time in Yellowstone when the rainbow trout had whirling disease that killed all the mature fish, hence, there were miniscule numbers in the main rivers. Although I loved fishing in some of those waters, the Madison in particular, the first river I floated down while fishing Yellowstone, there were scarcely any to no fish in it. So, even though I had my equipment, my map, and my compass to follow the right direction, without the guide there to continuously update me and let me know where I needed to fish and where I didn't, I would still be searching, looking for something that wasn't there.

Paraphrasing, Jesus Christ, the Guide "My Father has equipped you with what you need for the journey in life. He knows where you're going. Here is the Map. It is My Word. It tells you how to get there. Follow this Word, follow this Compass, The Holy Spirit that points you in the right direction, and then listen to Me. I will be with you for every step."

The Word of God, the Map, is no good if it is in your pocket or you are looking at it and cannot understand it, but the Guide will show you the way, and the Compass will keep your heading straight in order to get from point A to point B, start to finish.

"According to the map it looks good for hiking, but there's a bridge out, you can't go that way." While life's Map says, "That choice you are making is not a good one. The road is rough, full of detours, and dead-ends.

Therefore, the outfitter is only as good as his knowledge. Go to the source, the master of the environment, one able to instruct, having overcome the obstacle. Query one that's "been there done that" with a drawer full of T-shirts to prove it.

While we were in Yellowstone, the outfitter named Craig Matthews, had been documenting conditions of the water and environment, including temperature, depth, wind speed and precipitation; conditions of the fishing, including numbers, species and size of fish taken, date and time, the types of flies used, and a host of other facts every day for over 25 years. His lifetime of knowledge created a comprehensive diary of Yellowstone and its rivers. He has written many books. That is the kind of person to ask.

"What about this river?

"What about fishing here?

"What about flies? What is your choice?"

Not going to the one who has intimate knowledge leaves errant information void of wisdom and understanding gathered from first hand experiences. If you want to know about life, go to the creator of the universe. The title of His instruction book is one word simple: Bible.

While in Yellowstone, the guide offered little commentary on what we saw along the road in the park. He noticed very little, concentrating only at the task at hand; getting us to the water. Often being caught up in the journey in life to "the place" we want to go, leaves us with blinders on, not looking at what is around us. We just want to get to where we're going and get there, get there, get there. Yellowstone was more than getting from the hotel to the fishing hole ASAP! Every turn of the road was something different and exciting, something spectacular to see.

"Counting the days," "Waiting on vacation," forgetting about the rest of the year, or working in anticipation of the week-end forgetting about Monday through Friday leaves us missing out on most of the pilgrimage. There are 104 weekend days in a year, 260 weekdays, each one equally long, each one filled with opportunity, each one coming around only once.

CHAPTER FIVE
Parable of Life
from a Treestand Blind

Out of the car, into the woods, and Eric, close as a tick on a hound, had me remembering some of the things previously witnessed hunting during the early morning solitude, waiting and watching from the blind, thinking how closely deer hunting resembled life. More specifically how it imitates the difference between the true followers of Christ and non believers, as different as night is to day, and speaks volumes of how we see others, our view of God, and how God sees us in something as simple as a day in the woods.

Reflecting back on a typical morning, the first glimmer of light, adding slight color and detail, would start announcing the sun's appearing, before an explosive emergence in full glory on the horizon, like the prophets of old foretelling the coming of the Messiah, the Light of man before His arrival. Forever splitting the darkness covering man, bringing a new dawn out of the dark pit of despair, He burst forth with Truth and a clearly lit path, replacing doubt and confusion about which way to go on the journey in the emptiness. In the new light, the woods start to come alive, with the Light of the world, Jesus Christ, we come alive.

I remembered as the day became older the light emerged bolder, and illuminated details came into view ever clearer. The tops of the trees becoming clothed in pale pastels, once seen as a giant mass of dark grey, evolved into individual leaves, painted in vibrant colors. Contours and contrast once subtle or totally missing began to add character to the earlier thought flat terrain. Miles of floating, iridescent wisps of thinner than hair though stronger than steel spider webs, heavily laden with shimmering dew, dancing slowly in time with the slight breeze were revealed. In the new dawn, once perceived impenetrable continuous forest wall, an ominous Herculean glob, void of openings, gives in to uniquely distinct trees both large and small with structure and characteristics suited specifically to them; pine, oak, sweet gum, hickory, sassafras, maple, and many others, some good for shade or food, growing singly or in clusters, alive or dead, twisted, scarred, crooked, or straight; the details once obscured in the darkness becoming unveiled in dawn's light, make up a fraction of the brush strokes on God's canvas. Listening to what God had to say through the value of His creation was exciting, and I was eagerly waiting to discern the arriving splendor of a new day He had readied for Eric and me to uncover, from the vantage point "visible" from the "blind."

Aware of the obligation of a guide to teach and show, brought back thinking about that first time in Yellowstone, and how the outfitter had all the information and resources needed to complete our task, but it was still up to us to make the right decisions with the materials and knowledge given in order to have a successful journey. I started talking to Eric about the trail we were going to be using. We had already started part of the journey that morning by getting up early, having great fellowship and a hearty breakfast. Meat and bread with a little juice thrown in is always a nice start to making a great day!

It was a crisp, crystal clear, inky black morning, not a hint of moonlight visible save the fingernail appearing on the horizon. The stars took the liberty to show off, sporting a little more shine than usual it seemed, hanging overhead in plentitude, while Venus, "the morning star" continued her prominence inches above the tree line. With this beautiful backdrop we hopped out of the truck, got the gear together, and started walking through the woods.

I said "Eric, you know I know you've never been here, but I have and I'll show you the way."

"Well, that's good 'cause I couldn't find it without you."

"I could tell you how to get there, but that would only be as good as my instructions to you and your understanding them… but… I will take you there. I will be your guide."

(Similarly, discerning the Word of God can be utterly confounding, leading to misunderstanding and what seemingly known and thought true may not be true at all, unless you have someone, the Holy Spirit to correctly give understanding and direction.)

I told Eric "We're going to go a quarter mile or so and take the first fork on the left over the creek, around the bend, to the top of the hill and where the ditch comes across, hang a right to the deer blind. A blind is different than a tree stand. The deer cannot "see" into the blind. The true meaning of the danger is hidden from them."

He looked "deer in the headlights" puzzled. Those directions would be easy for me because I had been there, but for him they were clear as mud, he had no idea what I was talking about. He had never been there or seen any of that, and in the inky pitch-black, the visual clues would be nearly useless anyway. With light, Eric could at least try to find the way using some of the landmarks given, but in the dark, he would quickly discover all about him was black, indistinguishably opaque, and recognition absent.

Purposefully, I said, "That's the point. I'm going to take you there because I've been there. I know where we are going because I've been there before. You'll have to trust me. You'll have to have faith that I can get you from point A to point B, and that I know what I'm doing." I was becoming more "guidely" with every step.

Further, away from the sparse light of the field, the woods merged into a dark, eerie, unyielding barrier. We couldn't see anything except where, by our command, the flashlight would cast its beam of illumination. Even the familiar trail that I had made and used so many times before easily slipped away if concentration was lost while following the small amount of exposure emanating from the insignificant flashlight. And even though I knew where to go, sometimes the dark would play tricks with the distances from one place to another causing me to think I was one tree closer or a face level branch across our path was not where I thought, and was felt a little quicker than I remembered it should.

So we got to talking about following the light and without the light would be walking around in darkness. We could get there because I'd been there before, but the little pitfalls, snags, snares, briars, brambles and everything else that was in the way would be hidden in the dark. New things fallen on the trail, necessitating seeing to avoid a stumble were constant reminders of our dependence on the light, it's exposure was very inhibited, giving only a close, small focused, narrow view of things, washed-out and colorless, thereby limiting vision. The woods are beautiful, containing unbelievable colors and shapes. With the flashlight, however, all you can see is what is in front of your face, what you are focused on for a limited distance and perspective, and once the light discharged from the flashlight disappears, the woods metamorphose back into nothingness.

We walked on one step at a time and stumbled occasionally, bemoaning about how dark it was, even the moon failing us. Being the conscientious guide I would tell him "this, that, and the other," what I had seen at this place before, a general overview of where we were; however, with only the little bit of light, we missed the lions share of everything I was describing. All we could truly focus on was where our tiny little steps were going, with no other light; the missing pieces of the whole were invisible.

Well, we did make it to the deer "blind" as promised. Eric was thankful of that. "Not sure if I could find my way back, certainly not in the dark."

I told him it was easy. "You just go back there and follow the trail all the way back. Just the way we came, nothing to it!"

However, looking from his new perspective in the dark, with limited vision, would not allow enough detail to see how to get back. He had no idea where the trail was, but I did because I had been there before. Even though it was dark, I could have found the course, having seen it in the light; I knew what "the way" looked like.

In life, do not get advice from somebody who does not know. Don't walk around stumbling and falling living a dull and colorless existence in the darkness without The light. Jesus Christ is the Light and The Way, the one we ask. He has been there and knows everything, where we're going and what it takes to get there. In life, He is the one to follow, not wandering aimlessly with a little self-centered "flashlight" one-step at a time. Having seen the entire picture He knows exactly what is going to happen and how to get safely to the end.

Well, we entered the deer stand and settled into our nice comfortable chairs. I raised the curtains so we would be able to look outside unencumbered. Still pitch black we couldn't see anything, compelling Eric to use his flashlight. I didn't need mine; even in the dark I knew where everything had been arranged, where the chairs were, the best direction to look, and how to raise the curtains because I had built it.

It was very quiet and cold enough there were not any bugs. Emitted like a snorting bull through flared nostrils, steaming breath became visible by flashlight. Occasionally there was the monotonous droning of an overhead plane or far-off car, the wail of a sirened vehicle carrying precious cargo, but then, nothing. It was black and it was void. I thought this is how the whole world, all of creation started.

"The earth was void and without form; and darkness was on the face of the deep."

There was nothing: then… God spoke… and it all became real!

So we sat there and talked how that morning in the blind was like the beginning. Our journey was a parable, like life in a tree stand. We had made it a little way on our own and accomplished all we could to that point, sitting in the dark waiting and watching for the light of day, for life to wake up, for opportunity, for the goal. The rest of the events necessary in the hunt or life were out of our control.

While waiting, during the initial time in the "blind," Eric started relaying a story. An old saying came to mind. "If a tree falls in the woods and there is no one there to hear it, does it still make a noise?" The rendition of that saying in this setting, "If you have a Bone and Cricket moment and no one is there to witness it, should you tell it?" Of course Eric

151

did. Since I was not present at the incident, but heard it personally, straight from the source, I will paraphrase the incident as told by the intrepid one.

Eric awoke early one Saturday morning, as the story goes, and gazed outside at the beautiful setting cast before him: glorious sunrise, birds singing, and gentle breeze blowing….then he saw it! His arch nemesis, a buzz saw, tree destroying beaver.

"Ah ha!" He thought.

"I'll show him. That beaver's gnawed his last tree." In his socks and underwear Eric formed a plan.

"I have a bow."

(Eric told me his bow was red but several of his buddies and I agree it is DEFINITELY pink.)

"I'll sneak downstairs without waking Lori and Kaleb and deftly shoot that beaver."

Slowly creeping down the stairs in sock covered feet, he lost his footing. With his scantily clad, underwear covered butt, bouncing on each and every step, the descent ended much quicker than anticipated, though nonetheless, he remained undeterred from the mission. Quietly he gathered his beaver killing paraphernalia and hiding like a city boy, slouched on the deck, inching slowly toward the quarry. Now, like a Greek Olympian, he placed an arrow expertly on the string, drew back fully and….clank… the arrow fell onto the deck. Unflinching and resolute, he placed the arrow back, took another mighty draw, aimed, and zeroing in as if a hawk on a mouse, released the projectile of death. He followed the trajectory of the arrow as it skidded along the ground, bounced once, and lodged slightly in the beaver's backside.

Walking at a slightly accelerated snails pace while looking at the archer eye to eye mockingly, the beaver entered the water and swam away, the arrow visibly moving side to side like a bobber....Amazingly through great restraint I held back my laughter, opting instead to give consolation.

"I reckon' it might happen to anyone..." Knowing good and well it couldn't.

As we sat there it wasn't too long before we started to see just a little tiny bit of gray eeking out from around the shapes in the woods as tiny sunbeams started ever so slightly brightening the once raven sky, changing how we would see in the dark world. Like distant thunder, the low rumbling of a train with short blasts of its whistle echoing in the distance was interrupted by the maniacal caw, caw, cawing of crows. The rat-a-tat-tatting of a woodpecker searching for breakfast, caused a glance in time to watch spent leaves loosed from their hold by a jumping squirrel, helicoptering slowly downward as gravity beckoned them to rest. Another bird became vocal; quite far off, then close up, and then another, and another, with various songs, barking dogs, the staccato of clucking chickens and proud rooster crescendos filled the once hushed morning air.

As it got a little lighter, we could see in the blind. Eric said "Oh this has been painted on the inside."

"Yes it's been camouflaged so when the deer look, in they see only dark, not light wood contrasting our shape."

"That's pretty cool. Hey, this chair... It's green."

"Well no it's blue when the light becomes a little brighter, you'll be better able to see, but that's a pretty good guess."

So as we sat there I said "Watch as the world comes to life. Listen very carefully, very closely. You'll even be able to hear among other things, the wind."

He thought that was amusing to be able to hear something non-existent, as it was an absolutely windless day.

"As the sun comes up, as it gets brighter, yur fixin to hear clearly the wind in action, rustlin' the leaves, whilst causin' the faint swayin' of the tippy top branches. Listen to them birds. Certain types always seem ta wake up first and then others, addin'on to the early dawn choir. Blue Jays and Crows are among the early risers and most vocal of the birds in the woods. Their calls seem to reverberate over and over as their friends all gather up to join'em, seemingly squawk-in' about the intruders at a decibel level equal to one of them 747 arrow planes. You'll hear squirrels. The squirrels'll start comin' down out of their nests, makin' all kinda racket, commence to go barkin', hollerin', and chasin' each other, jumpin' from limb to limb, and runnin' through the woods actin'…. well squirrelly. You'll hear more and more; but more than hearin,' smell the smells of the woods comin' out as well.

"That wasn't me, Mr. Ron."

"That's not what I'm talking about!" As the sun heats things up, even the ground comes alive with musty, earthy smells. I didn't carry you up here from down yonder for grins. We're 'sposed to be observatin' a thing or two"

I was talking like that so Eric might more ably understand "what I was a sayin'" but it nearly exhausted me so I decided to talk more civilized like and try to learn him sumpthin uzin' my skills through examinin', examplin', and splainin'things what wuz in nature….

Mist from the frost burning off and evaporating in fanciful waves left a fresh cool tickle in our nose. Dripping onto the roof of the blind from the trees small droplets of water that only moments ago in the darkness were silent suspended ice clinging steadfast to the trees and leaves, continued to lend both sight and sound to the opening number of the orchestration of life unfolding before the senses. "Listen to the world coming alive from the tree stand."

So we sat there a little while and I said "Eric what do you see?"

"Oh this is cool. I see trees."

"Yeah, there's a lot of trees, we're in the woods! What else do you see?"

His hard thought reply, "A bunch of trees."

"Ooookay, that's good enough… for now."

We sat there a little longer; impatiently I had to press a little bit more. Querying gently as unto a kindergartener I said "Eric, what do you see now?"

"A whole bunch of trees!"

Now like pulling the answer from a preschooler, "Eric, come on, what more do you see?"

"I see some bushes …and trees."

"What kind of trees?"

"Well, I didn't think about that."

Finally, I had his attention. "Those are pine trees. That one with oak leaves… well, it's an oak tree. There's a sycamore down there close to the creek bed. There's a ton of sweet gum."

The ever increasing brightness of the light allowed us to begin to visualize details hidden under the veil of darkness.

"Look how clear it is right around this blind."

"Wow, that's pretty cool!"

Scholarly, I continued with renewed vigor. "The light brings focus and clarity to our vision, just like Christ brings clarity and vision into our lives."

So, not missin a lick while we sat there I said "Now, at anytime a deer may come by. That's what we've set for our goal this time. However, the journey… is what we are seeing, hearing and smelling. And THAT is what we came for."

Suddenly with a raised hand, conversation was halted. Whispering, "Did you hear that?"

Whispering back, "Yeah."

"That's probably a squirrel, but you never know. Let's listen." I explained to him that skill in listening was very important.

He said, "What did you say?"

"Eric, I can sleep in a thunderstorm, or when the grandfather clock chimes every fifteen minutes, and I've even been known to catch a little shut-eye at the ballpark watchin' the Braves, but while out here huntin'; whenever a deer snorts at me I immediately wake up!"

Sure enough, it was just a squirrel slowly working his way to within a couple feet of the blind. He looked at us and we looked at him, he kept on about his business, we kept to ours.

"Eric, now what do you see?"

"Well, there's more color. There are some bushes, green bushes."

"Yeah, as true light becomes available, the whole spectrum of color becomes visible. What about the shadows?"

"They're becoming less."

"Yep. Unlike today, the moon when full, casts ghostly bizarre shadows, everything in shades of gray and black making brambles, branches and holes constant adversaries. The moon, like the devil, is a look-alike, act-alike mimic. It tries to be like the sun, believing it has the same power, but it can only mirror something it is not, and gives false promises. If you had not seen the world before in the presence of true illumination, the Son of Man, it would look good, but the devil, like the moon, has false power, no warmth and only reflective light, absent of life giving power. In the darkness, both may look bright, but in the presence of True Light, as in the light of day, both flee. You can still walk around in moon light, although there is not much detail and no color. The black on black moon shadows are funny, they sorta look authentic, but they are a suggestion of a reflection of the real thing."

Then offered, "The shadows are nearly done, and the once muted colors of the trees and leaves are becoming more apparent. Look at the bark of the tree… Look at that tree there. It's got a vine growing on it. We couldn't see any of that when we first started looking." A little later, "It's pretty bright now isn't it?"

"Yes sir! I think it's really bright."

"But it's not full daylight yet. Every time we've looked we thought we'd seen all we were going to, but there's more to it. There's more day and light coming, but you have to wait."

"Sometimes we think we are seeing all there is in life but we have to wait a little bit to see what God has for us. We need to wait on His Light to show us the way. If you step out from the dark into the sun, you cannot open your eyes very much because it takes time, little by little by little, to accommodate to pure bright light. Similarly, we have to wait on the Light, on Christ, to work in our lives. We cannot go from emptiness of darkness into perfect Light all at once, or jump to the conclusion or skip ahead to the end of where we're going without DOING the journey…We have to wait. We see a little bit at a time and as more Light comes, we can see more, and move forward."

"What do you see now Eric?"

"I don't know. I hadn't done all that good so far, so that's my answer. I don't know. You tell me."

"Nope. It's not going to be that easy. We haven't seen our goal, so let's focus back to the journey. Look straight ahead. What did you see when we first got here?"

"Nothin'."

"What do you see now?"

"I see briars." Then, the wise one,

"What about that vine there with the tip on every briar lit up by the sun?"

The briars on a crown of thorns are yellow, and that morning with just the right angle of the sun, every briar was shining like a row of streetlamps. It was one of the miniscule, short lived events that could easily be passed over without careful attention to detail.

"It won't be there long because the light is changing. What we see will change. Our perspective will change." A little later I said "Now tell me what you see?"

"There's a hill there."

"Yeah, there's a hill there and one on the other side.

Had we started downhill without a flashlight we would have stumbled and fallen. There are a few sections where wash-out ruts and all kind of "going to snag you" things exist in wide sections. There's a swampy area earlier invisible to us but now fully exposed. Take a gander straight ahead and observe carefully what's in the trees. In the exact same place we looked only a little while ago, pine needles blown down are stuck in the limbs, clandestine details now exposed."

God is continually opening up our vision of details with the Light. In the blind and in life The Light continually opens our eyes so we can see more and more, not just "the woods", but separate trees, not people as a seven billion giant mass, but as individuals. With light come details from every tree, every person, and every branch, now seen from a new perspective, totally different.

We didn't see any deer that day but had an incredible "eye opening" journey of fellowship. On the way back it was as bright that day as it was going to get."What about now?"

"Well Mr. Ron," (he calls me that most of the time. Why? I reckon he figures I'm just old.) "I can see bugs flying. There are insects and some ants crawling on the deer blind in long rows. That's pretty cool."

"That's details of our journey that enrich the adventure. By the way, bugs and ants are insects. There is nothing here that was not here when we first arrived. The ants were up way before we got here. I saw them but that detail was only available at the time because of the flashlight. Look at the details God provided for us to make our journey so awesome. Do not simply look at a tree without "seeing" the bark; a bush, its leaves; a vine without noticing the variety: crown of thorns, honeysuckle, grape, muscadine or scuppernon, trumpet, ivy, or poison ivy, some are friends, others foe. Once you know the details of the individuals, whether people or in the woods, you can avoid the harsh consequences of the briars and poison, while enjoying the fragrance or fruit of the others, details only visible using the full effect of the light."

From the blind, the details of the woods were awesome. There was still more for us to see, not because we were waiting on the light, the light was already there, but in order to see more, we would have to continue our journey, take steps past what we could see from our "blind" spot. Without a step of faith we would only be able to see where we were and not where we were going. Each step leads forward in our journey. In the dark, our journey, our life, is fraught with "briars, brambles, and all manner of stumbling blocks." We can easily lose our direction and focus, altering, perhaps forever, our destination. Funny thing about it: The "briars and brambles and all manner of stumbling blocks" are present in the light. It's just that light steals their power. As with life, we can see to avoid or go around them still maintaining our focus on our course ahead. We can walk around aimlessly in the dark or choose the Light, and experience all God has to offer us in colorful, vivid, detail... One step at a time.

In the woods, there are trees; tree after tree after tree, but also in the woods, it is easy to navigate a destination by looking at the individual trees, not by looking at the forest but the trees. We can "see" in the forest because of the trees.

"Ah, this is the tree that's got that odd branch. There's that double tree... turn left at the double tree, go by the little bush that looks like an old man's beard, and bear to the right at the grapevine."

Certain trees are "evergreen," others, allow shade and shelter, a refuge perched high above the perils lurking beneath on the floor of the woods, some provide food and nesting habitat, fuel for fires and material for houses. Some are there seemingly for no other purpose than to enhance the beauty of the forest or give support to the others, sharing, and shielding the fierce storms that come their way-holding firm, strengthening the rooted foundations of others. But each tree is unique, each one is different. They are all trees, but each one has a purpose. You would not expect a tree failing to fulfill its purpose…..You would not expect to find acorns growing on a pine tree. God made each tree of the forest special, with purpose. As God's most prized creation, He created us each individually and with purpose like the trees…. But SO MUCH MORE!

"Eric, we can see only as far as our eyes allow, look right you see what's on the right, left what's left, or ahead only seeing immediately forward nothing of the periphery. In life we can see as far as we can see just for now, where we are and where we've been. We don't know where we are going or what tomorrow will bring. In order for us to see more we have to step out. If we want to see around the next hill we've got to get there, take a step of faith and go. There may be a deer just over that rise or something new waiting around the corner. We don't know until we start taking that step. Life changes. The only thing that does not change is God, and He is the Great Outfitter that supplies us with our needs and all that we need for our journey: He knows where we are going.

The hunt was over. The journey continued. Waiting for my mouth to be quiet, and since actions speak louder than words, we took a little hike and saw a lot of this and a little of that, identified an assortment of trees, tasted some sassafras, and saw a few more squirrels, things you might not notice if you are just "walking in life," but we were concentrating on walking in the light.

The talk soon centered around the concept of how the devil, the great deceiver, was like a hunter or fisherman, and man his quarry. Satan hides in wait, looking for a trophy, camouflaged so we cannot see him for what he is. He enjoys what he does and looks forward to it, often including some "friends." He knows our habits, habitats, and weaknesses, often using them to "seek and devour those he can destroy." Concealing the hook, or hiding the consequences, he temps us with lures, calls, and decoys that sound like, act like, or look like something they are not, and lets us wander close enough to fall into the snares, taken by his trap, or accept the bait so sinisterly and skillfully cast before us.

Life's Book of Knowledge enables us to uncover the devil, not listen to his calls, avoid the traps, and see the concealed hook… The Bible…. Need I say more?

CHAPTER SIX
Parable of the Trees

There was a big storm in Calhoun on a piece of property on the Oostanaula River. Even though I had not been there during the storm, the proof of its existence as evidenced by its destruction was obvious. Disappointed, I was heart-broken and sorrowful looking around seeing some of the ancient oaks that had been blown over. Impressively, they once stood straight and tall, appeared strong and powerful, sturdy and well built without any branches until very high up. They had faithfully produced acorns for many decades, provided much needed shelter, leaves for shade, nests for squirrels and birds, and occasional roosts for the turkeys. They had seen many storms and many, many seasons, the rings on the inside of the trees testifying to both good times and bad, of drought and flood, sparse and plenty, fire and ice. No one is alive now that was living when these trees emerged from the ground. I was saddened that first day while walking along the trail, noticing signs of wind and rain damage: busted limbs everywhere, leaves shredded; treetops, like spires once reaching toward heaven, were now sprawled in heaps on the ground, debris scattered haphazardly in every direction. Much of the forest I had grown accustomed was now littered with purposeless splintered pieces making travel hard and the usual path strange and difficult to find.

Upon returning to the area, I was a little less shocked at what seen this time, once overshadowed by the fallen wooden fortresses and going unnoticed until now were many other trees that seemed to be relatively unscathed. They had literally weathered the storm. Unfortunately, it seemed the trees left, still did not make as much impact as the ones that were "taken" by the storm. The scene reminded me of the story in the Bible of the shepherd searching in earnest for the one sheep that was lost, its value as precious as the other ninety-nine that were safe.

The first tree fallen that I really zeroed in on this second trip was a huge red oak. It was easily over a 100 feet tall and three feet thick, straight, and branchless for at least 40 feet, with massive, oversized limbs. On the outside of the tree, the bark looked normal, apparently perfect, and untouched. The tree once grew strong, straight, and stood tall, but lacking a firm foundation, now lay horizontal on the ground.

The roots, designed to project like the spokes of a wheel and penetrate the ground to supply sustenance and nourishment during good times and lean, were not as expected for such a large tree. Since it was easy to get water and nutrients from the fertile, moist river bottom, the roots were short, shallow and narrow, growing without the "need" to search long, deep, and wide. Roots are by design, supposed to "branch out" for nourishment and serve to anchor the tree. They gather the much-needed water supply to be stored anticipating drought, and if necessary, provide the tree with water for more than a year.

The tree grew up but not down, lacking foundational substance. When the storm came it was loosed from its base and life giving support, therefore destroyed. It no longer looked strong or alive. It had lost its life's purpose. It now was just a heap of lifeless wood to be consumed by worms and rot.

The second tree noticed was much like the first, also a colossal oak. As the other, the outside was intact looking like it should. This tree was remarkably different, however: the roots were massive, weighty, and strong, secured deeply within in the ground, a great foundation, but only by looking on the inside could you see why it had been twisted and broken in such a hideous manner by the storm. At about twenty feet, it was snapped like a twig and the trunk was split on one side, all the way back down to the ground. Hollow, it was shredded into a thousand splintery pieces held together top to bottom but separated just the same. Although the good foundation was strong, the tree was hollow on the inside. It had no inner strength and could not survive the storm.

The third type, actually represented by many, was very similar to the last two. A couple of these were even taller and larger, others puny in comparison to the fallen giants, but they all held resolute for some reason. Many of their branches were torn literally limb from limb. Tattered leaves scattered asunder, forced prematurely from their branches covered the ground. Tenacious in their stand, the foundations held and their trunks were solid, although scarred and battered they withstood the test of the storm.

A fourth tree I noticed was very different from the others. It still stood after the storm but it was dead and had been for a while. It still stood proud, but most of the branches had long been absent. It once was as tall as the other trees, but, although its beauty and substance were now absent, still had purpose. This tree was VERY dead, but told a different story: Even after dying, the tree continued to give. There were thousands of holes where bugs and woodpeckers had been. There were a couple birds on what little remained of the dead branches, and up at about thirty feet was a very large hole carved out and used by a squirrel as a nest, and on more than one occasion, an owl had taken up residence there.

What WAS the same was that all the trees had been exposed to this same storm. Heat, drought, floods, winds, ice, and many years and storms had called on them in the past. The ones standing were the ones that had good support, held fast by a firmly rooted foundation on the outside and a solid core on the inside; otherwise, they eventually would not and could not survive the storms. They couldn't simply "look strong" on the outside, the storm would reveal their weakness. The ones that had survived the storm held unwavering and true during the difficult times.

Battling daily, they strain to keep their massive weight standing upright toward the sky, defying the law of gravity, while the powers of nature lash-out from their inception trying to defeat them. Growing ever taller to compete for the life giving power of the sun, they stretch their giant leaf laden branches ever wider gathering lights energy to supply their need for fuel, covering the ground with a blanket of awesome shade in the summer, and supplying a mast crop of acorns that seasonally falls to the ground like rain, giving much needed nourishment for many of the animals that inhabit the forest. The easiest thing to do would be to give in to the daily battering, and fall. Some did.

I discovered there were many smaller trees looking just like their larger counterpart. No doubt some of these smaller look alikes were direct descendants of the impressive looking monster oaks, second, third and possibly a hundred

hundred generations represented by various sizes were surviving in close proximity.

But, I also noticed that when the trees fell they scarred, marred, and even destroyed some of the trees close to them. Some of the same trees from the same lineage, strong straight and beautiful were now busted and torn to shreds from the fall of the mighty tree. Some of the trees would not have fallen on their own save the influence of the bigger trees.... a graphic depiction. When the ones of influence and stature fell, the ones around them did not survive without being injured scarred or destroyed.

Appearing in the canopy, now forever changed, was a huge emptiness left by the collapsed "once greats" that would never be replaced in my or my children's lifetime.

I had been looking at the storm, how it affected and changed the trees, and how it influenced my view of that newly jumbled-up, tangled landscape. All the trees whether felled or upright had been through the exact same storms. Of paramount importance is understanding the parable of the trees.

The first tree represents a person that looks prosperous on the outside, appears to be doing all the right things, and growing strong. They probably attend church regularly, maybe sing in the choir or teach Sunday school, and would never do anything wrong in public that someone might see. Maintaining a certain persona, they are someone you would want to emulate. Watching how they are growing you want to be just like them. They do a lot of good things and provide for others. Appearing steadfast, they look every bit like they should, but when the storms come; prosperity and self-worth, achieving goals, or trying to gain more and more for "the look" they have worked so hard to maintain, outweighs their foundation. They have nothing for support, nothing to hold them up in times of trouble, during the storms of life, nothing to draw upon in times of spiritual, emotional, or physical drought. They fail. They fall.

The second tree represents a life that has a good foundation maybe even one that proclaims the gospel from a podium or classroom. Even at an early age knows and teaches, easily quotes scripture, teaches stories from the Bible, waxes eloquently when asked deep spiritual questions, faithfully tithes, openly gives wise counsel and tells others of their strong moral character, outwardly grounded in the Word while growing, knowing and telling. They do marvelous and wonderful things. However, on the inside there is emptiness and self-centeredness, caring more about appearances, substituting knowledge for wisdom, having no true faith, no true love, and no true strength. Even though the foundation is mighty and deep, there is emptiness. They are hollow. There is nothing of real value to support, and when the storms come they fall.

The third tree represents a life that stands firm on a good foundation. Faith leads to growth that will endure the storm. Resembling the others on the outside, like the others they keep on growing, statuesque and unshakeable continuously adding new roots, searching out the necessities for their existence. They aspire to live life more abundantly, founded in the Word. Even though the storms come and others fall, though they are battered, disfigured, and mangled, they cling to the foundation as it holds them fast and secure. They withstand it all as an example of inner power combined with a testimony of outward strength.

The fourth tree represents a life of enduring and persevering, a lifetime commitment that held fast through storm after storm after storm. Even when others around them were falling to the temptation to give up, give in, and quit, their stance was unyielding. Sometimes they were pummeled by the fierce winds of fear, sometimes the onslaught drought of disbelief and self-worthlessness, sometimes battling the torrential downpour of sickness and disease. Unyielding, in spite of being jeered at and mocked by others, some already fallen, they held their purchase, year after year making a stand. Bending but not breaking despite massive forces thrown at them trying to destroy them, faltering but not failing, crooked but not broken, incomplete and scarred, they survived as a testament to others. Their legacy lives on through generations. Even through death their steadfast commitments continue to give life in witness and in deed.

Like all of creation, we go through storms in life. Some are small and relatively harmless, others of "biblical proportions" are life altering and leave us beaten and battered. Only with a firm foundation, courageous faith and the strength it brings can we weather the storms. We falter and we bend…. or we fail and fall.

The storm never really was about the "storm." It was not about the trees, either. It WAS, however, about us. Looking at the trees and the lessons seen concerning the outcome from the storm are unquestionable…. I have pictures. The reality of needing strength coupled with a strong foundation is undeniably true.

God gave the illustration of life's truth using His power over nature under His control through the artwork he has exquisitely designed for us called creation. You can't look at the storm torn landscape and not see the Truth. You cannot offer denominational doctrine against it. The Truth stands without understanding of future events or Revelations. The Truth is undeniable and unwavering.

The Truth is about God.

The Truth is from God.

The Truth is God.

CHAPTER SEVEN
FINS, FEATHERS, & FUR
A Fellaship

Why Fins Feathers & Fur? Well, the simple answer is just to have Fun.

Enjoying the outdoors, going, looking, listening, hearing, and even smelling the creation God made.

The second reason and more importantly is Friends.

It's much more enjoyable enjoying outside or any-where with good friends, and is especially important to men. Jesus Christ, the all powerful, creator of the universe, chose twelve guys to have fellowship with and share in His ministry. He didn't NEED them, but by example showed us the importance of good fellowship with friends. They didn't sit around all day glum and quiet. The bible talks about activity and interaction. How joyful it must have been to journey with the omnipotent sustainer of the universe! Jesus and the twelve were true outdoorsmen with a love for the creation through experiencing the Creator. Some were fishermen. Often the Bible tells of cooking and campfires, journeys and adventure walking and talking. Christ taught them and shared with them the wonders of nature that He masterfully brought into existence with only a thought. He also gave them the equipment, map, and tools necessary for their, and our journey.

I have no Biblical or historical justification, but in my mind I can just hear them saying, "Matthew, you are one sorry fisherman!" My sister can fish better than you... always casting on the wrong side."

"Mark, you always catch the tiniest fish but brag about the one nobody saw that got away."

"Who put that sticky stuff in my sandals?"

"Peter, always the hot head. I guess going under the water instead of ON the water cooled you off a little!"

"Luke you might be a great physician but you surely can't cook!"

And so on. These were real men having great fellowship one with another. Along with these men, contained in the pages of this Book, are stories of faith and revelation, miraculous victories in battles against overwhelming forces, divine healings, marvelous teachings; and stories of ordinary men and women, through fellowship and commitment with God, doing extraordinary history changing deeds. It tells of God's divine plan for life's eternal journey, starting right now. Read the Bible, the greatest book ever written. It will FOREVER change your life.

The third and most important reason is Faith. Fins, Feathers & Fur or Fun with Friends & Faith. The three outdoor F's represent the other three F's and vice versa! Both require and lead to rich fellowship.

Why spoil a perfectly good time hangin' with your buds and bring up faith? Why is faith important? Why should we show our faith? Why do we share our faith? In one word…worship. We show our faith because we believe there is the omniscient, all powerful, awesome God that does EXACTLY what He says He will. He made a commitment to us, is faithful and just. He is unwavering in His Love commitment to us…His son Jesus Christ. He will never leave or forsake us no matter how many life's storms are thrown at us or how battered and bruised they leave us. His power is unending.

"How much power you talkin' 'bout?"

I am glad you asked. I once read if you were to purchase the energy contained in one cubic yard of the sun, the price would be staggering. If silver dollars were used, they would completely cover the earth. That's a lot of silver dollars! Did I also mention that the silver dollars would need to be stacked thirty miles high? That is silver dollars stacked one on top of the other completely covering the entire earth thirty miles high.

Now, OUR sun is very small in comparison to some others. It is actually teeny tiny relative to size and mass. As stars go, it is not particularly hot, only 10,000 degrees Fahrenheit! Water boils at 212. Paper ignites at 451. To me 10,000 degrees seems quite hot considering the sun is 93,000,000 miles away and on a summer in Georgia, temperatures rise to sizzle and beyond. You can "cook an egg on a rock" it seems so hot. Even though 10 thousand degrees at 93 million miles seems hot, scientists recorded some stars at 400,000 degrees. That takes one heck of a thermometer! And no, I do not know how they got close enough to measure how hot it was or who volunteered to do it!

The closest star to us other than the sun is Proxima Centauri at a distance of about 4.34 light-years away. It takes the light from our sun a tad over 8 minutes to reach us, although some people wrongly believe that it takes considerably longer at night! Considering that light travels 186,000 miles a second and our nearest star is more than four light years away, our nearest neighboring star resides 25.8 trillion miles away, give or take a few.

I also read that the new estimate for the number of stars in the "observable" universe is three hundred sextillion, and that doesn't count the planets, moons, comets, asteroids, or other matter... for that matter. You think that's a crazy number? It IS a crazy number! A sextillion is a trillion billion. That's a one with a whole wad of zeroes behind it, twenty one to be exact… and there's three hundred of 'em. Now if you were to count by billions to a sextillion you'd have to count a trillion of those billions.

"Aha." You say. "A trillion is bigger than a billion, lets count by them."

You probably couldn't count it in a lifetime, unless you cheated. Loosing track of where you were and having to start again, forget it! By trillions, you would then have to count a billion of those trillions. Let us say you counted one trillion every second, it would take you a billion seconds; non-stop counting for thirty-one years to reach one sextillion. A billion every second would take you a trillion seconds, non-stop counting for 31,688 years to reach the same sextillion. That is only one of the three hundred necessary. So multiplying leaves 9,300 years by trillions or 9,506,400 years by billions. Do you have any idea how many times your little piggies would have to go to market before you reach those numbers? Me neither. That's not the point, obviously, but I hope it gives an illustration of just how awesome the universe is.

The radius of the universe is purported to be 45.7 billion light years, diameter of 93 billion light years, and a volume of 410 nonillion cubic light years: 410,000,000,000,000,000,000,000,000,000,000 light years times 6,000,000,000,000 miles… in every direction, up, down, back, front, right, and so on and so on and so on…… You do that math! Couldn't see it in a lifetime… Not going to be any T-shirt saying "Been there. Done that…." Take more than those silver dollars you were saving to buy a cubic yard of our puny cold sun to purchase gas, especially at the prices these days.

But God created all the stars and the distances in between. Think about the power and the energy involved to create all the stars and the distance of the expanse of the heavens. Consider not only how much power it took to create it, but more so, the energy necessary to keep it in place: To keep it standing, keep it revolving, and keep it going. That's raw energy under control. That doesn't just happen by chance!

Creating fire is not a big deal, it seems. However, strike a match and then say to the flame, "Burn slow now. Not too hot. Not too bright." See how much control you have over that!

But as I think of how much power God has, unfathomable power, to create with a word a universe containing untold numbers of stars, providing incalculable heat and light, and keep it suspended in perfect order with just a thought, I also look at a tiny butterfly and admire the masterpiece of color, shape, and design. The contrast is striking: The frailty of the butterfly, how much finesse and love it takes to color it, versus how much power it takes to create the multitudes of stars and planets and keep them in place.

What about the sunset from our itty bitty sun. I have rarely witnessed a more spectacular sight or a more beautiful setting than admiring some of the sunsets or sunrises while traveling on a section of the Amazon, the largest river in the world, as it flows east to west. The radiating image emitted from the intense fireball constantly changes color and configuration in every direction, bright orange-yellow in the proximity, to rich dark blues, fading into purple farther out.

God could have created the night and day and left out the sunset. Every day at seven P.M., it could be "dark," Then, every morning at seven A.M. it would be "light." We wouldn't even know the difference. However, God in His love for us, decided to start the day, ending the night, with an unmatched display of color and glory; and, likewise, finish the day, beginning the night, as only He can. The exhibition of detail, that creation is not black and white but intricately thought out in rich vibrant colors is fully displayed awesomely with the sunset.

How much knowledge and care do you think it takes to have perfect control over snowflakes to make each and every one absolutely different? Think about Antarctica, Alaska, much less the world, wherever you look, the snow is piled hundreds of feet deep and not two snowflakes identical… That is power… That's majesty…That's God.

If you look at a Rembrandt, the style, colors, design, and signature are unique to him. There are books written about his life. You can know ABOUT Rembrandt, but he is long dead…you will never know him personally. Others have tried to copy him, mimicking the original very well, but they are fakes, nonetheless.

Go outside and look at the stars, think about how much power is represented, and then look around you at God's artwork. His signature and design are easily seen. Go sit in a deer stand, fish a river, hike in the mountains, or sit peacefully beachside and hear, see, smell, and feel the splendor and beauty of the ocean…. Stop, look, and listen. Taste, smell, and feel. When you go, purposefully see all of the things God created. He created them all for us. Not only did He bring creation into existence it for us, He created us in

His image so that we could understand and KNOW Him, not just ABOUT Him.

God's signature is the grand design of all creation, everything that was or is to be. With all His power, and all His might, He still cares more about us than any other part of His creation. He knows us intimately and wants us to have a relationship with Him. He shows us a little something of who He is through His creation. He shows us all of who He is by His love for us. He sent His Son to prove it.

Also, Fins, Feathers & Fur is about commitment, starting with our friends and families.

A lot of times we'll say "You want to do something?"

"Ah yeah, that would be great!"

Just like we started… "I'd love to." "That would be so much fun," but often we fail to DO. So, we lie to ourselves and we lie to our friends that we will do "Something" "Someday" but without following through, "Someday" never comes. It gets easier and easier to lie "in this way" to our family and friends with each "Someday" we utter. We tell our wives "I'll be happy to do that later, dear, just let me finish watching the game."

The problem is sometimes the game never ends. Not out and out bold face lies, as they say, but by not doing something or following through, we lie, nonetheless. The worst part about the behavior we've practiced time and time again on our friends and family is perfected in the "Later" "Someday" "Would love to" "In just a minute" answers to God…We lie to Him. We tell Him we are going to do something or we would love to do something… "Someday":

"That mission trip would be great. Maybe next year."

"Giving a tithe? Sure, next time we can, we're going to start giving our tithe."

"We're going active and start going to Sunday school as soon as the children aren't so busy with their stuff."

"SOMEDAY" We're going to witness to others and tell about this marvelous and mighty God we love so much. How awesome He is, How marvelous His creation, How matchless His love is for us. … When?!?

In this group, Fins, Feathers, and Fur, we hold each other accountable, plan things, put them down, and take the adventure. By mentoring each other, we are making sure we follow through and do what we say. Part of the time in the adventure is spent understanding that God gave us the outdoors to enjoy. Pushing our limits and each other, develops us, putting excitement back in our lives, making us more interesting and exciting to our families, friends and wives, and finding out more and more about ourselves and what God would have us do. "Someday" for us is now, through our commitment to each other and God in Fins, Feathers, and Fur, with the concept of "Fun with Friends in Faith." Having fellowship as a by-product, we are finding out more and more about His creation, how spectacular, and fascinating it is, and how much an awesome God loves us.

CHAPTER EIGHT
It is the Journey

What I've been learning over the years is that it's not about the end, the target, or hitting the mark. It is much more than any of that. It IS the journey. My son Joshua did more to teach me about spending time along the journey than anyone else. I am grateful to him for that and for adding so much more color so far in my journey. My wife and daughter as well, have given volumes more to my life's book being written day by day and year by year than I will ever be able to express, much less repay. I cherish each of the times with them and honor the memories, keeping them close and sharing the recollections. Some times are brought to mind by turning the pages of a photo album or flipping through "my pictures" stored on DVD. But most of the memories are recalled from deep within the recesses of my heart. The journey you take in life is exciting, just like being in the outdoors, there is always something new and something different. The results seen in the outdoor activities we do, mimic our journey called life. We're going to cast more than hook, hook more than catch, catch more than we keep. We are going to look more than aim, aim more than shoot, and shoot more than hit. I've never been on a fishing trip where one fish was enough. On the contrary "Just one more cast, one more try, just one more chance." One more, one more, one more. We are not satisfied with just one, and one more time, is never just that.

God created us for change. He created us for renewing. How many times has it been said, "I'm so full I'll never eat another bite." We've all said that, but that isn't true, and that's not the way we are built. We rarely have a one time experience and then let that last us. Doing so would relegate us to living in the past. By wanting, maybe needing, to cast "just one more time to one more fish" we can see an illustration about renewing our relationship with God, getting as excited about spending time with Him as we do about spending time with our friends and the outdoors, and sharing Him with others "like bait on a fishin' trip." Outdoor fellowship is simply another avenue to share with others the Creator of the universe, through sampling and exampling natural truths and personal experiences.

One more story to sorta' pull together the importance of experiencing the "Just enjoyin' the day pop. What about you?" part of the journey is very recent.

Eric Webster and I were hunting opening day of turkey season this past year. Like deer hunting, Eric had never been turkey hunting but thought it sounded like fun. We talked about it. A lot! We planned well in advance fortunately, since it took him forever to get his hunter safety card from Tennessee. This hunt, this adventure, this journey was a big thing. He bought camo for the hunt, including hat, gloves and facemask... He was serious!

All the way going to the property we talked "turkey". We talked about stories of turkeys and great hunts and hunters, what to expect, how turkeys will gobble at everything and the whole time we were excited. (Somehow I forgot to mention my early calling experience with the cows, but I doubt he would have understood). It WAS exciting! During breakfast we talked some more turkey!

Hunting out of a blind with some decoys that day was a good thing since the prediction was "heavily overcast skies with a 100 percent chance of rain." I never really understood how there could be a "chance of rain" if it was going to rain for 100 percent certain. Why not just fess up and say "It's going to rain?"

Anyway, with the first clap of thunder, the turkeys gobbled. At breakfast, we had talked about turkeys gobbling when it thundered.

"You see the turkeys gobbled."

An owl hooted. The turkeys gobbled. Everything talked about on the way seemed to be taking place. The turkeys gobbled when the geese came honking noisily over the river. They gobbled at a blue heron that was squawking down on the river. I'd call and they'd gobble, I'd call and they'd gobble, back and forth it went. It would thunder and they would gobble. That morning, the toms were plentiful and loud. They were gobbling for all they were worth, showing their strength, and trying to gain dominance, one over the other. A hen came by really, really close. She'd cluck and I'd call, she'd cluck, neck stretched toward the sky, and I'd answer. Shortly after, a jake came by, but quickly skirted around the decoys knowing he wasn't as big as the tom displayed out there, realizing the date he was hoping for just wasn't worth it! The tom was fake but the Jake didn't know it, just knew it was bigger than he was, so he kept his distance, and kept his mouth slam tight shut, never made even as much as a peep. All we talked about was coming into play. We were having a great morning! Thunder roared, lighting flashed and the rain came, and every time it would thunder, the turkeys gobbled.

I continued calling as we sat and two toms came just from our left. They were coming quickly to a combination of my (expert of course) calling, the voluptuous rubberized hen, and that big ole tom decoy. They were coming after that tom and eyeballing that sexy hen! I'd call and they'd gobble, I'd call and they'd gobble, as they got closer…, closer…, and closer.

Whispering to Eric, "Just like we talked about in the car, you take the one left I'll take the one on the right, or you take the first one I'll take the second one, however it works out. I'll count to three and then we'll shoot." The two toms continued a beeline course to the decoys, a few yards from us.

I counted quietly so not to be heard by the "two toms on a mission," but easily loud enough to be heard by Eric "1…2…3".

Nothing happened. Eric didn't shoot. I looked over at Eric. He was just staring. The turkeys were within inches of the decoys, too close to keep the fakes a secret any longer and we had to shoot.

"Shoot Eric! Shoooooot," escaped in puzzled tone from my mouth, the surreal scene unfolding before my eyes, seemingly in slow motion as my gun sounded with a hurried and very poorly aimed blast.

Well, Eric shot three times at two turkeys in five seconds while less than forty yards away at the max. They didn't run. I thought we had hit one, or thought I at least had, because it was flopping around.

"Good," I thought…

Well not so good. They were fighting, not dying, and they nonchalantly walked around. Eric's three times at two turkeys five seconds and forty yards away left them STILL walking around. Like thunder, he'd shot, they'd gobbled. He shot. They gobbled. He shot. They'd gobbled, with no idea we were even shooting at them! Of course, that tells a lot about Eric's shooting ability…. I was too stunned to shoot any more, and asked Eric why he didn't shoot on the predetermined count of three.

"They went behind the grass."

"Behind the grass? You have a 12 gage automatic shotgun with special turkey bustin' shells. They were in full strut at spittin' distance and you didn't take the shot…the first shot… go ahead and take the first shot, shot… at the two toms I so expertly called up, I might add….. Because they went behind some grass…..? Really!?!"

Besides that, the whole trip, the whole morning was one incredible journey. We didn't take a bird that day. We should have I understand, probably two, but we didn't. It was the journey not the outcome that made the day great. We had been had, that day: had a blast, (Eric had three) had fun, had fellowship, and had created a new story that had to be told.

Obviously, I will refabricate it more; and more readily than Eric….somehow, his wife knew about it before he got home! A perfect morning, a perfect day, thunder and lighting didn't matter. We took a great adventure, hopefully a non repeatable outcome, and had a grand experience, but we "didn't get to take the prize," some people would say. I beg to differ. I say we got the prize we just didn't get to "take" a turkey, but taking the journey is what makes the difference. That's what Fins, Feathers and Fur is about, a journey of Fun with Friends in Faith through fellowship, understanding each other and what God does for us.

CHAPTER NINE
Opening Day

Outdoors, our journey often ends at another hunt completed or seasons' last day. In life, our earthly journey ends at death, but truly only begins for believers. The last grand adventure and fellowship is face to face with Jesus Christ. Like going on a noteworthy adventure outdoors, we look forward to it, we plan for it. We know part of what it is going to be like, but not exactly what is going to take place or when. The excitement and full understanding of life hidden from us, known only by God, the ultimate outfitter, makes it the supreme adventure.

I have talked some about Dr. Harvey Howell and he certainly was one of the men who mentored me in the outdoors. He really was quite amazing with some of the stories he had in his repertoire and some of the things others, including Miss Lonnie, his wife told that he had done as a small boy, even as an adult. When I first met him, I was about fourteen and he was probably in his forties. Wes was a couple years younger than me so it wasn't until he was about fourteen or fifteen, it seemed, that he was able to go do some "grownup" hunting with Dr. Harvey. I do remember Wes wearing some wing foot type shoes once. I must say that was the first and last session for Wes to take to the woods in "go to meetin'" shoes.

Deer season always opened on Saturday. On Sunday afternoon, the day following the opening of deer season one year I was working as an orderly when Dr. Harvey caught me in the hall and approached, inquiring, "Well boy, did you go hunting?"

Reluctantly, "No Dr. Harvey it was kind of rainy and cold…ah, I just didn't feel like getting up, I was kind of sorry this morning. We had a football game Friday, I didn't get home 'til late and I just was tired…."

He looked at me kind of quizzically with a shade of near disgust on his face and very pointedly said "Son, a man's only got so many opening days."

I thought it was kind of funny at the time, but the more I thought about it… the more I think about it, and over the years it has become one of my favorite sayings to ponder over. It isn't the "been sorry and not gone hunting" on my part that kept me thinking. It is more than hunting or fishing opening day or even the anticipation of another season. It's about the days we have. Those days will only open up for us so many times.

"A man only has so many opening days" is so profound.

Yes, we look forward to seasons: opening day of turkey season, deer season, dove season, trout season or others. Each season brings us closer and closer to our last season, to our last opening day, and whether it is hunting, spending time with family or even work, our days are numbered. Our time is measured and short.

What are we going to do with these days? Are we going to miss out, thinking we have plenty of time, and blow our last opening day, our last opportunity; or get up and make preparation for the things we need to do? Are we going to "Someday, Later, Love to" only to find there are no more days?

"I'll tell them I love them."

"I'll encourage them."

"I'll give them a hug."

"I'll call them."

"I'll dance with her….later."

Our opening days are numbered. Our LAST opening day only comes around once.

Several years ago I had the opportunity to go hog hunting with Dr. Harvey, Wes and a couple other guys. It was on New Year' Day. New Year's Day was on a Monday or Tuesday that year. They usually went hog hunting every Sunday. I didn't go on Sundays, but I got to go on this particular hunt.

The dogs we used were bulldogs, called catch dogs. When you got "on a hog" the bulldogs would be turned loose and catch it. Somebody would tie the mouth shut, which wasn't me, thankfully. Somebody would hold the back legs of the hog and raise it up, which sometimes was me. The other people got stuck holding the dogs, really trying to hold the dogs off the hog…that usually was my job. It wasn't a very fun job but none of the other jobs were either.

One of man's best friends was a dog that would try to find the hog by smell, upon finding the hog, he would start barking or baying with a very distinct sound. When the bay dog was heard is when the bulldogs would be turned loose, proceed to the bay and the fight ensued. To perform your pre appointed task would require you to run as fast as you could to keep track of the melee, ultimately getting to the scene of snarling, squealing, barking, chaos as soon as possible.

We were hiking up the back of Pine Log Mountain and about three quarters of the way up Dr. Harvey stepped over to the side of one of the ridges and said, "Hold on boys. I believe I hear the bay dog."

Wes looked at Dr. Harvey and looked at me and said "Uncle Harvey you thought you heard the bay dog at this spot the last time we climbed up here."

Dr. Harvey kind of laughed and said rather sheepishly "Yeah boys, I didn't hear the dogs. I'm just tired and I think you boys need a rest."

I was glad he was tired. I sure would have "heard" the bay dog a lot sooner if I knew that was all it took to get a rest. Of course no one would ever admit to the others that they were the one that was tired, but that ploy was as good as any I had ever heard. At that point and time Dr. Harvey still had a lot of opening days left. He had had many in the past, and more to go, but I was struck with interest that his opening days were getting shorter and shorter, and coming around more often it seemed, just like mine, but he was not going to admit it. We never want to admit that we don't have a lot of days left, but sometimes we don't.

The apostle Paul when writing to Timothy in 2 Timothy 4:21 said "Do your utmost to come before winter." Paul was in prison for his stand proclaiming the Good News of the saving power of Jesus Christ. Paul could stay steadfast, because of his unchanging, unshakeable, confidence in what he believed. Imprisoned, soon to be executed Paul would finish the journey in the direction he was headed. Imploring Timothy to come before winter was important to Paul. It would require a major decision on the part of Timothy. If Timothy did not come before winter, the journey would not be possible, the port would be closed and passage unobtainable. Also, if he did not come before winter, he would have no other chance for fellowship with his friend and teacher.

Paul's life here, nearly over, was in the final season; "winter" was fast approaching. Paul would shortly be put to death. While in the dark, damp dungeon of a prison, Paul continued to exhort and uplift his friends and fellow believers, continuing in fellowship, living each day for a purpose, enduring all for the sake of the journey he had been guided through, fully outfitted to complete the task by the Master of the universe. He had started poorly, a "religious" leader, a zealot, a murderer, then; forever changed and in 2 Timothy 4:7 Paul says it all "I have fought the good fight, I have finished the race, I have kept the faith."

With winter closing in, Paul's earthly journey would be complete. Our winter is coming, for some it is already here…..come before winter.

I met a guy at work the other day. I'm going to say that his name was Dennis. Dennis was going for an MRI and I was going to assist by giving him some sedation. Dennis had been in a submarine training unit while in the service, and went through some intensive indoctrination in preparation for a tour of duty aboard the sub. Due in part to this, he had claustrophobia pretty bad, and could not stand close quarters.

Dennis was going to have a brain scan, so I got involved to help. I went up to the room prior to the procedure to gather information and meet him, nearly bumping into him at the door. Actually, he was on his way out to the hall.

He said "Hi my name is Dennis. I don't remember things very well, but I'm going to have a brain scan."

I introduced myself and he said "Hi my name is Dennis. I don't remember things very well, but I'm going to have a brain scan. I remember things that happened a long time ago, but my short term memory is just about gone."

"Hi my name is Dennis I'm going to have a brain scan. My visions gotten to where I can't see very well either but I'm going to have a brain scan here in just a little bit."

He asked me my name and I told him my name again and he introduced himself again as Dennis.

He said "Now my eyes aren't that good. I've got this brain tumor in my head and it's got my eyes going and my short term memory is not very good either, but it looks like on your hat that you have some flies."

I had an OR hat made of some material with pictures of fishing flies on it. One of the ladies that worked with us had made it for me since she knew I liked to fish.

I told Dennis "Yes they are flies, mostly trout flies."

That really excited Dennis and got us into further conversation. He said "Do you like to fish?"

"Sure I do."

"Boy I like to fish, too. I really like to fly fish. Um, you like to fly fish?"

"Yes I do."

"Well, my name is Dennis and I like to fly fish. It looks like you have flies on your hat."

"Yes. That's what they are."

"I use to fly fish a lot. My best fly fishing partner and best friend is my wife, but my wife's not doing very well, she's kind of sick."

I had ready the history on Dennis and I knew his wife had already died, he just couldn't remember. She'd been ill for a while and died about two weeks before he got severely sick. So, we talked about fish a little bit and he continued to tell me about his love for fishing. Finished with his MRI and back in the room I stayed and spent a little more time with

Dennis. Again he told me his name and he liked to fly fish. He could remember all the old things; he just could not remember what he had said earlier or some of the new things in his life. But he said "We have a place on the Etowah River. Did you ever fish the Etowah River?"

"Yes."

"Well we have this trailer up there and we really love to fly fish. My wife and I would go, she's my best friend and my best fly fishing partner. We'd go fishing a lot up there. We'd just spend time in the camper and go out and fish. Boy I love to go fishing! I love fly fishing! We'd catch some fish, we would cook some fish, and we'd camp, and we'd fish and do it some more. That's some of my best memories with my best friend and my best fishing partner. I really loved that." He said, "Where do you like to fish?"

I named a few places. "I like Yellowstone. I love fishing the White River." Thinking and talking about our favorite place to fish, I continued. "Well you know Dennis I guess my favorite place to fish is wherever I'm fishing. You can dream about going to exotic places and all, but wherever you're fishing, wherever you are, is what you ought to enjoy."

I thought in life it's the same way. We can dream about our vacation. We can dream about when we retire. That is fine, but we should focus on what we are doing now, every moment in the journey we're on, that's what we should enjoy.

"Maybe I'll get to go to Alaska or Chile…. goodness so many places….."

You can't just sit around and plan, then wait and

wait and wait on that one small part of the journey and be satisfied. It is experiencing getting from here to there, fishing where you are, living where you are, not some mystical place you can't wait to go to. Don't hurry, hurry, hurry, the days waiting "until vacation, until I retire," because you will miss out on all the things along the way. While fishing in the Jacks River sometimes, we would come up on some good ole boys and they'd have fished all the big holes. They'd fish one big hole then run up and go to the next hole, next hole, next hole. But, we'd fish in between because we knew there were fish in there. We knew it wasn't just the big holes, but the prize was found in going steadily steady, little by little. We'd fish all the holes not just from one spot to the next, and most often catch way more fish because they missed the details. They missed the journey in "catching the fish." They were only interested in jumping from one big thing to the next, not enjoying in the rest of the opportunities and time.

Well, it got time for me to go and do something else. Dennis said "You know I really enjoy talking to you and I really love fishing. I think what I'm going to do is tomorrow… I'm gonna go fishin'. I love fishing with my wife. Yep, that's what I'm going to do. Tomorrow, I'm just goin' fishin' with my wife.

I knew he would never go fishing again and it was sad to me because he had such a passion for fishing, shadowed only by the passion for his wife: his best friend and fishing partner and that was awesome. It really got me thinking. I wonder what would've happened if Dennis had known the last day he went with his wife would be the last time he would go with his wife, and that the last time he stepped out of the water would be his last step out of the water, the last cast he took would be his very last and he would never again, ever, get to experience the things he loved, and spoke so passionately about…."just goin' fishin' with my wife."

We don't like to think about our final cast. We don't like to think about our last shot of the night or the last day of the season, but they are coming, we're all going there. A man's only got so many opening days. He's only got so much time when he has influence over his family, or friends, to make a difference, to make an impact. God gave us the days, the beauty of His creation. In His word, He gave us a target after the journey is over. We never know when our last day is going to be over. The last time that we'll say "I love you." Our last time with our friends, or our family. Our last cast for the last try at the last fish, but everyday we're closer and closer. Sadly, Dr. Harvey has no more days, by now it has been a few years; some other friends of mine are out of days as well. Mine are short and getting shorter, and the opportunity for Boone & Crockett or Bone & Crickets are dwindling. We have to make the best and the most of what we have left. For some of us it's a long time, others short, but it's not about jumping to the end, it's about the journey and fellowship and the things we can do to mentor and teach young men and women, sons and daughters. Through the outdoors we can easily see what an awesome and mighty God we have and serve, and all the things that He has done just for us, the extreme details… just for us. How much time do we have left? I don't know.

Winter fast approaches…
Our last season, our last chance, our final choice…
COME BEFORE WINTER…
A man's only got so many opening days.

Conclusion

What I have learned from situations or sayings, not in order of importance.

THE TOP TEN

1.   "Pride comes before the fall"...."Pride comes before the fall"...."Pride comes before the fall."

2.   "Pride comes before the fall".... "Pride comes before the fall"...."Pride comes before the fall."

3.   "Darkness is shattered by a little bit of light"....While caving (spelunking) we would often turn off all the lights. It was darker than black. You would have to be careful when moving your hand closer and closer trying to see it, not to poke out your eye. We would light a match to a candle and through its shimmering yellow glow see each other illuminated amidst our surroundings. From a deer stand a little bit of sunshine peeking over the horizon changes shadows and ominous shapes into recognizable landscapes and life. The Light of God, Jesus Christ changes the world around us into beautiful colors and details, gives hope, allows the "blind to see", and shines bright our path until the journey here is completed.

4.   "Come before winter".... Our time is short. We are all getting closer to "winter," our last season, a time of slowing down, darkness and death. Winter can also be a time of great joy if you have harvested "riches" from past seasons to fill the storehouse in lean times. These "riches" cannot be bought for any price, fortune or fame, are accumulated abundantly during "fun with friends in faith through fellowship" and cannot be destroyed by moth or rust. Fellowship with Jesus Christ supplies "riches" beyond measure overflowing the storehouse, to be shared by ten, one hundred, or a thousand fold, and winter has no power.

5.   "Just keep to the right"....If we go off following directions that are based on erroneous information even if we follow those directions with precision, we will not end our journey in the place we thought we

were heading . In the outdoors or in our direction in life we must ascertain with certainty that the information we are following is true to the mark. We must follow the Guide that is knowledgeable for the journey and knows where the path leads.

6.   "I'm just enjoyin' the day pops. What about you?"...I realized with this little statement that many times I was wasting the blessings that were right in front of me while speeding past them on my way to "the finish". The times we have to fellowship are precious and limited. My son and I used to be able to spend most of every day together. As time passed we started to have to schedule time that he and I could spend on a one on one basis, hiking, fishing, talking, camping, and enjoying our journey together, concentrating on deeply knowing each other. Sometimes we would go to an exotic place like Yellowstone or Arkansas, duck hunting. Sometimes we'd just go hang out around the campfire. We had many, many journeys as a family but Joshua and I needed time together for fellowship that only comes to fruition through cultivation of time spent together. Even during these times I must admit often the journey was not savored as much as it should have been by me. There is a song "Cats in the Cradle" that illustrates what happens way too frequently in our relationships with our family, friends, or God. We must keep our eyes open and experience the journey before it passes us by on the way to "the finish".

7.   "I'd love to".... "One day".... "Sounds like fun".... "That would be fun".... All are synonymous with something that is not going to happen without a commitment. I hear these statements a lot. I even get reassurances sometimes like "You can count on me!" "I'll definitely be there." "Sometime we will"....They will, sometime. They want to, sometime. The problem is: it's always just sometime else. Without a commitment in our lives we will end up somewhere "sometime." It's just not where or when our family or friends need us.

8.   "A man's only got so many opening days"....Our days are numbered. Our seasons are few. The Bible says our life is like a vapor and then it's gone. We are here to make a difference. Take time to stop along the journey and enjoy life. Many times we want to hurry one "bad"

day up to get past it only to be frustrated by how quickly the "good" day, "good" time, "good" experience comes and then vanishes. Each day is a gift. We don't know when the last day of our last season will be. If we did, we would want "Just one more". Live each day like it is your last. Take that dance with your wife. Tell someone you love them. Better yet show someone you love them. What will your last opening day look like?

9.   "Our circumstances don't determine WHO we are"....But erupting forth from us is in response to situations encountered along our journey, the true essence of our being is made manifest by the choices we make. We can choose to slow down, detour, or stop our journey whenever it becomes difficult. We can wander around aimlessly in the dark, struggling as if going uphill against a strong wind. We can allow an obstacle to block our way; or we can persevere, push forward, following the Map, Compass, and Guide. We may change our direction if necessary if the route is crooked; while holding true to the path, keeping our eyes focused forward on what lies ahead, and not looking back. In a race, it's not how we start but how we finish that gives victory. Our journey, our race toward the prize, starts with the first steps we take. It ends with the last one. Making our way back and finishing strong is what life is all about. We can be beaten and fall, concede and stay down.... or rise up and continue the fight. We can perish in the dark or choose the Light of Salvation. My choice is the latter for every option. It's your choice, too. Make a choice choice, and choose wisely. You'll thank yourself for it in the end.

10.   Pride comes before the fall....There is a theme I've picked up on along my journey. Simply stated: "Pride comes before the fall". We often overestimate our abilities or attributes. We soon learn that we need others. Most of my Boone and Crockett/Bone and Cricket moments have resulted from someone, myself included, getting way too close to the precipice on Prides Mountain before a little help from our friends nudge us over the edge falling ever downward until, as Yoda might say, "The bottom we reach"....... "Need me to shoot that deer for you." Maybe you need to borrow a bullet." "Huh, Watch this!" "This is how a real man does it", etc. Many of these memorable moments along the journey are, however, created purely unassisted by ourselves without intervention

from our so called friends. Mostly we're just too proud to admit it."Must be something wrong with the fishin' pole". "I think I hear the dogs barking". "I can shoot deer, I've always shot deer". "All you gotta do is set the hook, "and so on. The higher up we lift ourselves, the further it is back down to normalcy. Sometimes it would be better to just lay low for a little while, get comfortable and enjoy the rest, 'cause sure 'nuff we'll be right back down there... again!

Epilogue: More Than The Hunt

My heart is racing. It's cold out, but I feel the rush of adrenaline so I don't notice. Every breath through my nostrils produces a visible fog. I can smell the aroma of sausage as it sizzles in our guide's frying pan. Breakfast is almost ready. I look to my left and see my son, Corey. His friend Joshua is huddled next to him. I also see Scott and Tim, two close friends that I have enjoyed hunting and fishing with on many occasions. Ron, the author of this book, is there, too. He, like Scott and Tim are not related to me, but they are as close as brothers. On my right sits Brian. He is a long time friend and fishing partner. I'm glad to get to experience his first duck hunt with him. We are in the blind for three days of duck hunting. At daybreak, just as we see the first flight of ducks break the horizon, our guide calls out, "Boys, your breakfast is ready!" I have to pause and give thanks to God. I am truly a blessed man.

Our three-day hunt was very successful. The ducks were flying, and we brought home plenty of them. Ron claimed to hit two ducks for every shot, boasting that he killed them all! That is a slight exaggeration, but not uncommon when you hunt with a group like these guys. I have hunted for many years. I enjoy calling and hunting ducks, catching fish, and killing a deer, but the real satisfaction in these times is not the hunting or fishing. Over three days, I got to spend quality time with my son, and some men that, in military terms, I would want in my foxhole during a battle. Sure, we hunted. But we also ate some great food, laughed (a lot), studied God's Word, and talked about things that really matter in life. I guess you could say we hunted with a purpose! My life is full because of times like these, hunting and fishing with close brothers.

Hunting and fishing are both great opportunities to get away and invest in relationships that matter. I find that through these times, my relationship with God is deepened, and my relationships with others are strengthened. We live in such a fast-paced world, that many times it is easy to miss the relationship that God wants to have with us. When we miss that relationship, we don't experience the true relationships He wants us to have with others. Even Jesus Christ made time to retreat, recharge, spend time with His disciples, and focus on the important matters in life. The disciples changed the world because their purpose was defined through a journey they experienced with Jesus. He wants us to experience the same life-changing journey.

In Ephesians 5:15-17, Paul wrote, "Be very careful how you live – not as unwise but as wise – making the most of every opportunity, because the days are evil. Therefore, do not be foolish, but understand what the Lord's will is." According to these verses, we have a decision to make everyday. So many times, we make plans with friends, yet never carry them out, missing some great opportunities for fellowship. Our duck hunts happen because, first of all, we understand that it's more than the hunt we're planning. We know that these trips will impact our lives. Our lifelong journey with God is the same way. We have to make it a priority. We have to be intentional about it. Maybe you are at the point of decision about joining God on the incredible journey He has planned for you. Don't wait. The decision to give God your life is the best decision you'll ever make.

As I write this, we are in the final stages of planning our next duck hunt. I am excited about the adventure. Our group has grown by two, and we are really hoping for a great hunt. Even if we don't see a duck, we will have a great time because it is about more than just the hunt.

Steve McCombs
Missions Pastor

For more information or to contact someone :
dhattaway@tabernaclebaptist.org
smccombs@tabernaclebaptist.org   or
http://www.tabernaclebaptist.org/

Maybe you have a Boone and Crockett or Bone and Cricket escapade or a story of fellowship with friends in faith you'd like to share with others. If so, send them along with name age and city or state to ronwoodwardFFFF@yahoo.com. With enough of them, a book sequel of your stories might be just the encouragement someone else needs. I already have four more and my friends are continuously "making me proud" generating others.

Maybe you just want to know more about starting your own Fins, Feathers, and Fur group or men's ministry. I would love to know about it, pray about it, and encourage you in that as well.